A Spacio

Published by
The Bible Reading Fellowship
15 The Chambers, Vineyard
Abingdon OX14 3FE
United Kingdom
Tel: +44 (0)1865 319700
Email: enquiries@brf.org.uk
Website: www.brf.org.uk
BRF is a Registered Charity

ISBN 978 1 84101 605 4
First published 2012
10 9 8 7 6 5 4 3 2 1 0
All rights reserved

Acknowledgments
Unless otherwise stated, scripture quotations are taken from the Holy Bible, New International Version, copyright © 1973, 1978, 1984 by International Bible Society, and are used by permission of Hodder & Stoughton Publishers, a member of the Hachette Livre Group UK. All rights reserved. 'NIV' is a registered trademark of International Bible Society. UK trademark number 1448790.

Scripture quotations taken from The New Revised Standard Version of the Bible, Anglicised Edition, copyright © 1989, 1995 by the Division of Christian Education of the National Council of the Churches of Christ in the United States of America, are used by permission. All rights reserved.

The Living Bible copyright © 1971 by Tyndale House Publishers.

The paper used in the production of this publication was supplied by mills that source their raw materials from sustainably managed forests. Soy-based inks were used in its printing and the laminate film is biodegradable.

A catalogue record for this book is available from the British Library

Printed in Singapore by Craft Print International Ltd

A Spacious Place

Alie Stibbe

CONTEMPLATING THE SECOND HALF OF LIFE

Contents

Foreword

In this era of virtually limitless choice, there is one area of our lives in which we have no choice whatsoever—ageing. The question is, do we fight the process or welcome it with grace, equanimity, serenity and aplomb? This is where Alie Stibbe's guide to 'the second half of life' is an absolute must for all women who want to live and enjoy, not just accept, the inevitable.

With a perception that challenges the limitations we unwittingly accept, insights to Bible stories that are revelatory, and practical questions that exercise our minds and spirits, Alie invites us to follow her on her own journey through highs and lows to a place in midlife that, for all of us, is as liberating as it is surprising. No more sighs as I look in the mirror and lament what is past. I've always said so tritely, 'The best is yet to come.' Now, thanks to Alie, I know that it is.

Michele Guinness

Introduction

The Lord was my support.
He brought me out into a spacious place;
he rescued me because he delighted in me.

Psalm 18:18–19 (NIV)

Sitting at the table in our sunny conservatory, looking out over the beginnings of my potager garden at the back of our first 'proper' home, I marvel at how the landscape of my life has changed in the last ten years. My first book, *Barefoot in the Kitchen: Bible readings and reflections for mothers* (BRF, 2004), drew on my experiences from the intensive years of parenting a family of four small children, my healing and journey of recovery from post-natal depression, my acceptance of life 'stuck at home' and my search for God in the ordinariness of everyday domesticity. Essentially, that book drew a line under the first four decades of my life. Since its publication I have been encouraged by the number of women who have contacted me to say that they found the book a help in their own difficult times. Over the years I have often been asked to speak on the subject of finding God in the ordinary, but that has become more challenging as time has gone by. Life moves on, and the years of parenting young children recede into the past faster than you realise they can when you are up to your elbows in buckets of soiled terry nappies or covered in PVA glue and glitter. My children are now almost all grown up and ready to leave home: one has left and come back several times. I am no longer 'chained to the kitchen sink' and no longer a vicar's wife. I am a first-time home buyer and I have gone back to work full-time.

As my life is now so different, a female MBA graduate acquaintance of mine suggested that I should follow up *Barefoot in the Kitchen* with *Barefoot in the Boardroom*! Although I was the director of a one-woman 'kitchen-table-top company' while my older children were in their early teens and still needed me at home, I did not (and still do not) work at boardroom level in the sense that she would understand it. Consequently, this book, written as I face up to the stark reality of my 50th birthday, has been christened somewhat differently as *A Spacious Place*.

A Spacious Place is a set of five reflections aimed at helping Christian women take stock of the past, re-evaluate the present and look ahead to the future as they face the second half of life and all the challenges and opportunities that it will hold. My hope is that the book will be especially valuable to those who consider themselves one of the large number of women, myself included, who belong to the generation emerging from the '15-year parenting paradigm'[1] to find the world a very different place from the one they inhabited a dress size or more ago. Those women can be left wondering what on earth happened and what they should do now. Midlife is a time when women begin to ask questions that they did not have the time or energy to ask during their child-rearing years. It is a time when the superficial externals of life become less important than the inner spiritual journey for meaning and purpose. Maybe this book can be a springboard enabling the reader to start to address these questions in a context of faith, without sidestepping the myriad thorny issues that line the way.

I decided to call this book *A Spacious Place* because that is how I see the second half of life. It's a time when there is more room for all the things that were put on hold for child-rearing, when some of them, at least, can be rediscovered and begin to develop into their full potential, and a time to think about taking up something completely new. I came across the phrase about three years ago when my own life hit a major crossroads. Although I had written about coping with change for a magazine article several years previously,[2] nothing had adequately prepared me for what I was about to face—but more about that later.

Trying to prepare for what I thought might lie ahead, I began to meditate on a sermon entitled 'The year of the gate' that my husband, Mark, had preached at the beginning of 2008, a year that was to precipitate momentous change in both our lives. We had a scholar of Hebrew staying with us at that time, and she pointed out to me that the Hebrew word *chai*, meaning 'life', is made up of two symbols: *yod*, which symbolises 'God' or 'the Holy Spirit' and has a numerical value of 10, and *chet*, which is in the shape of a gate and has the numerical value of 8. In Hebrew thought, the number 8 is symbolic of 'new beginnings', which is something we often associate with the idea of an 'open gate' or 'going through a gate'—hence the title of Mark's new-year sermon for 2008. The scholar went on to tell me that the word 'life' ('the gate to God' or 'the gate through which the Spirit flows') thus has a numerical value of 18 $(8+10=18)$.[3] She mentioned that this numerical value provided a link to Psalm 18:19. I can't remember what reason she gave (a lot has happened in the last two years and the notes I made in January 2008 have faded in the sun that has streamed through the study window since then) but Psalm 18:19 reads, 'He brought me out into a spacious place; he rescued me because he delighted in me.'

I loved the thought of 'a spacious place'. The term seemed so full of promise, and I had been waiting so long for my so-called big break in life, now that the children did not need me so much. I started to dig a bit deeper.[4] I began examining the Hebrew word *merhab*, meaning 'a spacious place', more closely by looking at all its occurrences in the Old Testament. Most of the verses in which it is used are similar and can be summed up by the two that follow:

They confronted me in the day of my disaster, but the Lord was my support. He brought me out into a spacious place; he rescued me because he delighted in me. (Psalm 18:18–19; also 2 Samuel 22:19–20)

But those who suffer he delivers in their suffering; he speaks to them in their affliction. 'He is wooing you from the jaws of distress to a spacious place free from restriction, to the comfort of your table laden with choice food.' (Job 36:15–16)

In each instance there is the idea of being moved from a place of suffering or distress to a spacious place. Rummaging further, I found out that the word 'distress' in both contexts has the connotation of 'a confined space' or 'a narrow space'.[5] So these verses are describing a situation where there is movement from a narrow place to a spacious place, from a place of restriction to a place where there is freedom to grow and flourish.

This reminds me of the pepper plants I grew from seeds that I saved when slicing a red pepper for a stir-fry this spring. Amazed that the seeds germinated at all, as they grew, I kept potting them on into bigger and bigger pots. Now ten of them stand two feet tall in large pots on my conservatory windowsills and they are even beginning to flower. Weeks ago, though, I took some surplus seedlings to work, to share with others. One colleague left her seedlings on the window ledge by her desk in the small pots they had come in. She watered them, but that was all. When I left for my summer break yesterday, those seedlings were still two inches tall and had put out no extra leaves. They were still confined in 'a narrow place'. They had warmth, water and light but no room to grow.

Being in a spacious place is like allowing God to pot us on, just as I potted on my pepper plants. Our roots may be disturbed as we are placed in successively bigger pots, but that is a necessary preface to having room to fulfil our true potential. I am excited about what that might mean for each of us in the years ahead.

Taking my word search even further, I found myself in Exodus 3. This surprised me, as the same chapter had been my starting place for *Barefoot in the Kitchen*. It is the passage where God speaks to Moses from the burning bush: '"Do not come any closer," God said. "Take off your sandals, for the place where you are standing is holy ground"' (Exodus 3:5).

I made much of Moses taking off his shoes in front of the burning bush as God used an ordinary object to gain his attention and speak life-changing truth into his life. I explored how, by treating our kitchens as holy ground, we might be able to enter God's presence through the ordinariness of domestic life rather than allowing ourselves to be dragged down by the negative connotations of being 'barefoot and pregnant in the kitchen'.[6]

In *Barefoot in the Kitchen*, I'd stopped reading at Exodus 3:5. Reading further now, to verse 8, I noticed not only the mention of 'a good and spacious land' but also the repetition of the idea of being moved from a place of suffering to a place of blessing: 'Moses hid his face, because he was afraid to look at God. The Lord said, "I have indeed seen the misery of my people in Egypt... I have come down to rescue them from the hand of the Egyptians and to bring them up out of that land into a good and spacious land"' (vv. 6–8).

Surely, finding myself back in Exodus 3 while at a crossroads, about to move beyond being 'barefoot in the kitchen' to understand the spiritual meaning behind the term 'a spacious place', had to be more than a coincidence?

Discussing my findings with my husband, I was told that the Hebrew word for 'Egypt' (*mitzrayim*) echoes the word for 'narrow places' (*meitzarim*).[7] So Egypt was 'a narrow place' or a place of confinement for the Hebrew slaves, and the Lord had promised to lead them to 'a spacious place' or a place of freedom. Throughout time and across all continents, oppressed people groups have used the exodus story as a source of inspiration, finding in it the strength to leave their 'narrow place' and make a treacherous journey—literally or metaphorically—to the 'spacious place' promised to them by God.[8] Women at midlife also face a similar transition, and that transition can be very daunting for those who have invested all their time and energy in raising their children.

Some of you may be thinking that I am going to stretch the metaphor by implying that our years at home with young children are our personal 'Egypt' and that our families are the 'slave drivers' inflicting 'misery' on poor old us until God miraculously breaks into our lives and leads us out of domestic captivity into a new life of freedom and promise! You could read that meaning into the metaphor if you so desired, but personally I believe that investing in our children is the most valuable legacy we can leave. My intention has never been to undermine the importance of family life or to devalue the decision that many women make to stay at home as full-time mums. All I wanted to express in my first book is that some women, myself included, found mothering young children very difficult: it was 'a narrow place', a place of restriction, but one in which we could find spiritual meaning and fulfilment if we consciously chose to do so while that period of life lasted.

An inevitable consequence of the fact that children grow up, spread their wings and leave home is that our lives do eventually become emptier. We can find ourselves in a literal 'spacious place' as a result of children leaving *of their own accord*. We don't need to rebel against motherhood or re-enact our own exodus: in the end, children usually leave, and there is not much we can do about it except to live creatively in response to that spacious place, just as we tried to live positively in response to the narrow place. Rather than focusing on the attitude of 'Whoopee! Now I'm free to do what I like at last' or even wallowing in the more negative emotions associated with 'empty nest syndrome', I see the term 'a spacious place' as a metaphor for a transition into a phase of life where we have the time and opportunity to become all that God wants us to be.

On a more serious note, I do believe that, for Moses, there was a connection between taking off his shoes on holy ground, ready to listen and obey the Lord, and being prepared and able to lead the people of Israel out of Egypt to the borders of the promised land. Might it be, therefore, that we are better prepared to make the transition from the 'narrow place' of being a stay-at-home mum into the 'spacious place' of our promised future if we have already learned the difficult but valuable lesson of being barefoot in the kitchen?

I ended *Barefoot in the Kitchen* with reference to Hosea 2:15: 'I will... make the Valley of Achor a door of hope', so I suppose it is natural that the next phase of this spiritual journey is to move from that narrow valley to the open, fertile pasture that awaits us. Nevertheless, moving from one place to another is not always easy. Moving on takes a conscious decision and then action. Many people do not realise that they can make their decision by making no decision at all. We can camp at the crossroads of life, like Terah, the father of Abraham, who left Ur but never reached Canaan because he got stuck at the literal crossroads where the camel trains met at Haran (Genesis 11:31–32), or we can be brave and move out of familiar territory into the new things that await us, as Abraham did after his father died. So I urge you to 'go through the gate', following the leading of the Holy Spirit, to make the decision to 'choose life' (Deuteronomy 30:19) and spend some time with me, trying to identify what lies before us and grasping it firmly with both hands.

In the following chapters, I ask and try to answer the kind of questions that we may find ourselves asking as we think about living in the spacious place that we trust holds fulfilment and satisfaction for the next part of life. These chapters are an open journal, an exploration of my thoughts and experiences as I have wrestled with God through several years of questioning and change. My situation and experiences may be different from yours, but I am sure there will be places where you can identify something of yourself. Underneath our superficial differences, I have found that we women are more similar in our hopes and fears than we are willing to admit. On that note I begin this book, as I ended the last one, with an expression of the desire that the Lord will prepare you and me for all that he has prepared for us.

To this end we always pray... asking that our God will make [us] worthy of his call and will fulfil by his power every good resolve and work of faith, so that the name of our Lord Jesus may be glorified in [us], and [us] in him, according to the grace of our God and the Lord Jesus Christ. (2 Thessalonians 1:11–12, NRSV)

Chapter One

Looking the past in the eye

I will remember the deeds of the Lord;
yes, I will remember your miracles of long ago.
I will meditate on all your works
and consider all your mighty deeds.

Psalm 77:11–12

I woke in a panic this morning, unsure if I was dreaming or in fact struggling to come to terms with a real tangle of events. I was leaving work with a colleague, but from an unfamiliar venue—we must have been on a training day or something— and I could not remember where I had chained my bicycle. Had I left it outside our usual office building? Had I left it in the vicinity of the training venue? Or had I left it somewhere seemingly more convenient to the route home from this unfamiliar place? I couldn't remember. I tried to stay cool and think. No luck. What to do? Go back to the office? Go home and hope for the best?

As I forced myself into consciousness, I realised with grati- tude that I was really at home in bed. I calmed myself and tried to think back over the past week, to remember where I had been and figure out where my bike might be. That in itself was not easy: the task made me panic. It had been a very unusual week. On Friday I drove my son seven miles to school because the bus did not stop to pick him up. I came home, parked the car, collected my bike and went to work—

late, but I did go. Thursday was normal, but I forgot my bike lock and had to carry my bike up to the office landing to keep it safe all day. On Wednesday I went to work but came home at lunch time to host a meal for one of the college departments. Then we all walked into town to look at the new college building, after which I walked home in the rain. Tuesday I was off work, so no biking. Monday was normal: go to work, chain up bike, work, unchain bike and then come home on it. Logically, I realised, the bike must be in the hall downstairs—then I remembered seeing my daughter come home from a party on it as I was drawing the curtains before bed. What a relief!

This doesn't just happen in my dreams. I can be in an important meeting and forget a word, a room number, a course code or the name of a member of staff. That makes me feel idiotic and incompetent. In a time of funding cuts in further education, when people are being made redundant all around me, the last thing I want to be seen to be doing is losing my marbles at work. Yet it is a well-documented fact that failing memory is common in midlife. Forty per cent of midlife women report forgetfulness. Those who suffer with hot flushes find things worse: research has linked these flushes to an increase in what is called 'poor verbal memory'.[1] Unfortunately, this kind of short-term memory loss is also related to interrupted sleep, so, if you have hot flushes all night and can't sleep, then you can't expect to be on top of things at work the next day. Not good news for a data-handler like me!

Being unable to remember things worries me in regard to my past. There was a time when I could tell you where we had been on holiday each summer of our married life, but I can't any more. I can figure it out from landmark holidays if I try, but the information is no longer at my fingertips.

Thankfully, I am assured that this kind of memory loss is due more to information overload and stress than to oestrogen loss, interrupted sleep or hot flushes.[2] So why do I worry about it? Essentially because 'to be ourselves we must *have* ourselves—possess, if need be re-possess, our life stories… [because we] need such a narrative, a continuous inner narrative, to maintain [our] identity, [our] self'.[3] If I can't remember my past, I have no genuine idea who I am right now. I also have less chance of figuring out what I want in my future, since it is commonly acknowledged that 'the source of hope is memory'[4] and 'memory is the instrument we trust to guide us'.[5]

At the crossroads that midlife presents, with the challenges and choices it places before us, it is not very easy to move forward into the potential spacious place that this period of life offers without first looking back, remembering where we have come from and what we have been through so that we can make sense of our past. This dynamic is unavoidable, as we grow most productively through the process of reflection followed by action.[6] I believe that women can avert or, at least, reduce the severity of a potential midlife crisis by taking time to reflect, evaluate their past and produce some kind of order out of their actions. Obviously there are certain facts about our past that are immutable, but the rest of our experience provides a multitude of mosaic tiles that we can arrange in many varieties of patterns, each pattern creating its own particular meaning.[7] How we choose to arrange those tiles and tell our story will determine how we understand the path of our lives up to the present moment. Rearrange the pattern, putting a different tile in the centre, and you can come up with a whole different story. This is because 'our autobiographies are not literal translations of life, but artistic constructions, works of self-interpretation… that focus on representative events or ways of acting and which confer some kind of order over time'.[8]

Take what happened to me three summers ago, as an example. I had finished writing up my PhD thesis at University College London and had been encouraged to apply for a postgraduate research fellowship. That period of my life concluded with a variety of stressful events telescoped into one rollercoaster week. I passed my PhD exam on the Monday, obtained a glowing reference from my external examiner on the Tuesday, submitted it to the grant-awarding body on the Wednesday, and then heard I had been unsuccessful in my application for the research fellowship on the Friday. Three years later, I am working as a timetabling officer with a data administration and audit function at our local college of further education. Ordering my interpretation of events one way, I could say that I am a failed academic who did not manage to achieve her ambition of becoming an established lecturer at one of the best universities in the country. Alternatively, I could rearrange the pieces and say that I have successfully reinvented myself after an interesting period of postgraduate study and now work in a challenging environment with the opportunity for career progression. It is a choice between seeing the glass half empty (which I am very good at) or seeing the glass half full—which, I am learning, is the better option.

As Christians, the focus around which we arrange the pieces that make up the patterns of our lives should be the understanding that God has an overarching purpose for us, not only as a community of faith but also as individuals. Only with God in the mix are we able to glimpse the true pattern and meaning of all that lies behind us, and I would be bold enough to say that his default position is to see the glass half full rather than half empty. If we believe in the promises in the Bible, we know that 'all the days ordained for [us] were written in [his] book before one of them came to be' (Psalm 139:16). God tells us, 'I know the plans I have for you. They are plans for good and not for evil, to give you a future and a hope' (Jeremiah 29:11, LB). If that is true, then everything that has happened in the days behind us must have an upside, as will everything we have yet to experience in the days that remain ahead of us. Thus, God-centred remembering is 'vital when it comes to the shaping experiences of our faith' because it helps us understand who we are and who we are likely to become.[9]

Remembering what the Lord had done was, and still is, an essential part of the construction of the identity of the Jewish people. The command to remember occurs frequently and insistently in the Bible, as we read in Moses' speech before he died: 'Only be careful, and watch yourselves closely so that you do not forget the things your eyes have seen or let them slip from your heart as long as you live' (Deuteronomy 4:9). The events they are exhorted to remember are 'the watershed moments where God reaches a hand to aid his people'.[10] Time after time, we come across passages in the Bible that tell how God did this and God did that (see, for example, Deuteronomy 32; Psalm 105). As a young Christian, I found these passages second in the list of boring things to read, after the lists of who 'begat' whom. Now I understand how important they were in defining a people's identity and, subsequently, the identity of the individuals concerned. What is true for the Jewish people is also true for us: remembering those watershed moments when God reached into our lives forms our identity and helps us to avoid the sin of believing that what has happened to us is of our own doing or merely the hand of fate.

Sometimes it is good to take time to do some deliberate remembering. Just before the birth of our fourth child, I had the opportunity to take three days out to attend a silent retreat for women. One of the spiritual exercises the retreat leader encouraged us to do was to look back so that we could look forward. We were instructed to take a piece of A4 paper and fold it in half three times, forming eight squares once the paper was opened out. Then we were asked to draw or write in each of the first seven squares something representing seven key moments in which the Lord had spoken to us and guided us in our past. The result would form a kind of illustrated map of our spiritual journey to date. Once this was complete, we were to go away into the gardens of the retreat house, find somewhere quiet and ask the Lord what he would have us write or draw in the empty eighth space. We were also to bring back something that represented what we had heard, so that we could place it on the chapel altar and commit the next step of our lives to the Lord.

I went into the garden and sat under a beautiful *Spirea* bush, commonly known as 'bridal wreath'. As I listened for the Lord in a silence punctuated only by bird song and the chirping of grasshoppers, I was led to Song of Songs 2:10: 'Arise, my darling, my beautiful one, and come with me.' Although I was one week away from becoming a mother of four children under the age of five years, I sensed that a new season of life was about to begin, in which I was going to get my turn to 'go to the ball'. I picked a small branch of *Spirea*— the 'burning bush' out of which God spoke to me, if you like—and put it on the chapel altar to signify my willingness for whatever I was to 'come away' into with the Lord.

Within six months of my return from the retreat, we had moved from Yorkshire to Hertfordshire. My husband began a new phase of ministry, but there seemed to be no role for me in the church to which he had been called: the congregation was filled with many talented people, one of whom told me quietly but firmly to 'go home and look after my children'. I had wanted to get involved as I had been before, but it was obviously not going to happen. After a tussle with some inevitable feelings of rejection, I realised that this was the opportunity to identify the special something into which I felt the Lord was calling me 'to come away'. As a result of stocktaking in my life, I identified the fact that I had wanted to study languages rather than science when I was at school. Now was the time to redress that omission. But which language? A visit to Norway just prior to our move to Hertfordshire had inadvertently started an incredible series of events, too complicated to describe in detail. The next eight years were a special time when I really did get to 'go to the ball'. By summer 2007, I found myself with four grown children, an MA in Advanced Scandinavian Translation and a PhD in Scandinavian Studies.

I then hoped for a second chance at a career in academia— but, as I mentioned at the beginning of this chapter, it was not to be. I must admit I was devastated. I thought the ball was over, the golden coach had reverted to a pumpkin, and the mice that had been white horses had run back under the skirting board, leaving me standing back where I started—in a different kitchen, yes, but this time wearing rather frumpy slippers, fit for aching middle-aged feet, rather than being a lithe, barefoot 30-something.

In an attempt to ward off a backward slide into self-pity, I decided to repeat the exercise from the 1996 retreat and look back to look forward, because I was at a major crossroads. I took a piece of A4 paper and retired to the comparative quiet of the bedroom. I dutifully folded the paper three times to make my eight squares and asked the Lord to help me remember the key points in my spiritual journey since I had scribbled Song of Songs 2:10 on that other piece of A4 paper, which I had kept by my attic desk for over a decade. I was unable to fill all of the squares, but I managed to put something in most of them.

In the first square I drew the open door described in Revelation 3:8: 'See, I have placed before you an open door that no one can shut.' This was the verse that the Lord had used to speak to me as I recovered from post-natal depression in the late 1980s, when he promised me a door of hope in the Valley of Achor (or Valley of Tears, Hosea 2:15), but it had become a renewed promise that my desire to study a foreign language, which emerged in the late 1990s, was the beginning of a process that even some very adverse situations were not going to stop. That indeed proved to be the case. Somehow or other, I was provided with funding for my studies, sometimes from freelance work but eventually with a scholarship and a government research grant. Starting as a short course student and ending up as a graduate student on a PhD programme, I saw that the open door was certainly not shut in terms of my studies.

In the second square, I wrote out 1 Corinthians 1:8–9: 'He will keep you strong to the end, so that you will be blameless on the day of our Lord Jesus Christ. God, who has called you into fellowship with his Son Jesus Christ our Lord, is faithful.' In my mind, this has always read, 'He will keep you strong to the end… He who has called you is faithful [and he will do it].' I also noted down Revelation 2:3: 'You have persevered and endured hardships for my name, and have not grown weary.' These verses kept me hanging on through my studies when my husband was signed off sick for three months on two different occasions, through financial difficulties at home and through the many excruciatingly painful experiences of having strong-minded teenage children who were determined to rebel against vicarage life.

In the third square of my A4 page, I wrote out Daniel 1:4–5. These verses describe how Daniel was selected to be taught the language and literature of a foreign nation and how he was assigned a daily amount of food and wine from the king's table during his three years' training. They became very meaningful to me in 2003, when it became clear that one of our children could no longer stay at the local secondary school. No other local school within driving distance could offer a place. Eventually a place became available at a regular secondary school that was too far away for a daily commute, but it had boarding provision. Coming from a public school background, I was amazed that such an institution even existed, but where was the money for the boarding fees to come from? I either had to give up my studies and return to work to find the money or be awarded a research grant so that I could continue to study and use the grant to help cover the boarding fees. Like Daniel, I felt I had become a captive (in a metaphorical sense, mind you), learning the language and literature of a very unfamiliar nation. I dared to take the words of Daniel 1:5 as an indication that I would be awarded the research fees and maintenance grant—and indeed I was. The Lord was very faithful over the years when I was studying, in so many ways.

My fourth square contained Isaiah 30:15: 'This is what the Sovereign Lord, the Holy One of Israel, says: "In repentance and rest is your salvation, in quietness and trust is your strength, but you would have none of it."' I feel quite embarrassed to share this square with you, but it represents the importance of learning not to put your own interpretation into what the Lord is trying to say to you! Let me explain. After I had submitted my PhD thesis in April 2007, the plan was to have the summer months free to recover and catch up with the family and several years' worth of outstanding chores before I started on the hoped-for research fellow-ship. Rest was very much on my agenda—in line with the verse that I felt God was emphasising. As it turned out, I worked all summer as a personal assistant because, deep down, I was unable to trust the Lord to provide the funds we needed for the son who was about to start university that autumn. Yet, by the end of the summer he had managed to earn and put aside all the funds he needed and had no need of my intervention. I had not rested, my work had been unnecessary and my anticipated plans were down the chute. Contrary to the advice in Isaiah 30:15, I was not quiet and I was not trusting: my inner being was in turmoil after losing the research fellowship. It was not a happy time. I had been offered the chance to take a real rest, but I would have none of it. I was struggling to make things happen in my own strength and blaming God when they did not work out the way I wanted.

The fifth square contained Psalm 18:19: 'He brought me out into a spacious place; he rescued me because he delighted in me.' All that summer I had understood 'the spacious place' in this verse as a metaphor for the fulfilment I would find working at a prestigious academic institution. How wrong I had been! In fact, not until four years later have I finally understood that the Lord has brought me out into a spacious place—but a place very different from the one I had imagined. I have found a level of contentment and acceptance that I could never have predicted. I actually believe that losing the research fellowship was God's 'rescue' plan, and I am happy to think that this was because 'he delights in me'—just as he delights in each one of us. Over the course of the last four years, we have put a child through university, established a charitable trust, liquidated a business, found and bought a house, left parish ministry and begun a new life in a town near the village that was home for twelve years. I could not have done all that if I was commuting to London each day to a pressurised job in a top-notch university—a job that actually would have run its course in three years and left me unemployed with a mortgage to pay. Although we may not admit it at the time, looking back, we can see that God knew best all the time.

Putting the latest piece of A4 next to the original piece from the 1996 retreat, I can see the map of my Christian life from 1972 to 2007, and I have given you a hint as to how it turned out in the years since then. It also shows me that it is probably time for another bout of remembering. Looking back like this gives us an opportunity to see the pattern that is woven by the Holy Spirit across the years of our lives: 'A life's record with God in the details can be a spiritual feast for our souls. When we count our blessings on paper, our gratitude soars. It is all so evident.'[11] It helps me to realise that there is purpose and direction in everything that has happened to me, and gives me the chance to understand who I am as a woman of faith, even if that faith has been wavering at times. When we are plugging away at the minutiae of everyday life, it can be impossible to see the wood for the trees. Without knowing it, we can be wandering aimlessly in ever-decreasing circles, unless we find our way to higher ground and have the chance to peer out across the tree-tops. Only then can we stop, look back and see the full vista of the terrain over which we have come, and perhaps get a glimpse of the way ahead.

Perhaps this exercise of reviewing our life's journey with God becomes more crucial as we face the second half of life. The first time I 'remembered what the Lord had done' in my life back in 1996, there was more of time ahead of me than behind me. I think I still felt the same when I did my second conscious remembering of my 'faith story' in 2007. Now it is the opposite: facing the approach of my 50th birthday, I realise that there is more time behind me than ahead. I do not have time to dither about and waste what is left. It is time to stop and look back again so that I can put my disappointments behind me and make the most of the future.

I have often joked with friends that my PhD was my mid-life crisis, because it seemed such an unusual thing to do in my situation. Now I believe that it was not the crisis I made it out to be. My crisis was the three years following the award of my doctorate, when I did not know what was coming next career-wise, when I had a confused understanding of the true meaning of success, when (as a result of my career disappointment) I began to ask big questions about the existence of God and the meaning of life, when I followed through but questioned the wisdom of my husband's step out of the apparent security of parish ministry, when I had to face up to rediscovering who I was if I wasn't a vicar's wife, when I realised I was gaining weight and physically fraying at the edges... and the list goes on. I very much identified with Dante's comment in *The Divine Comedy*: 'Midway upon the journey of my life I found myself in a dark wood, where the right way was lost.'[12]

My current circumstances and the need to complete this book have precipitated a minor time of remembering. At the time of writing, we have been out of parish ministry and living in our own home for almost two years. A succession of episodes in which water has come pouring through the kitchen ceiling from the bathroom above has awoken me to the fact that this is 'real' life now and that we have to deal with it. There is no Diocesan Estates Officer to ring in an emergency, yet somehow it is refreshingly liberating. My husband is enjoying his new job. The charitable trust he runs is doing well and it is comforting to know that the leap of faith we took was the right one. I have been in full-time employment in the public sector for almost four years with the same employer and have a job of some responsibility. I am ten minutes' walk from work, still on hand if there is an emergency at home, not exhausted after a daily commute into the city, and we have enough to meet the bills. Having 'enough' is an answer to the prayer I prayed as we left parish ministry: 'Give me neither poverty nor riches, but give me only my daily bread. Otherwise, I may have too much and disown you and say, "Who is the Lord?" Or I may become poor and steal, and so dishonour the name of my God' (Proverbs 30:8–9).

The final three squares on my last piece of folded A4 paper are still empty, but, in a sense, they have been filled because the verses that came to me in 2007 now have newer and fuller meanings than they did then. Isaiah 30:15, 'In repentance and rest is your salvation, in quietness and trust is your strength', has been a key verse for the last 18 months. After we left parish ministry, I found that I was exhausted, but this time I listened and accepted the permission to rest and find salvation after 25 years of service. The Lord tells us 'where to stop and rest' (Psalm 139:3, LB), and I have done so.

That aside, the last twelve months have also been a time of questioning. Questioning is not always a bad thing. My faith has been renewed through that period of struggle and doubt because, ultimately, my source of hope has been in remembering God's faithfulness in the past and being assured of the same in the future. Strangely enough, as write this book, I find that the questioning is over and I can say that I am experiencing the 'salvation' that comes not just from the 'rest' prescribed in Isaiah 30:15 but also from 'repentance'. Repentance means having your life turned around. For me, that has meant the slow shedding of the expectations I felt were placed on me in parish life to have the kind of spirituality that suited each of the churches we worked in over the years. Now I am getting back in touch with the personal faith of my childhood, which is more simple and reflective. Now the major aspects of the transition we have been through as a family are almost over, and, although I do not know what lies ahead, I have come to a place where I can honestly say I know and experience the fact that 'in quietness and trust is our strength'.

The scriptures command us to remember, to bring our past—individual and corporate—into the present, so that we do not forget who are, where we have come from and, most importantly, what the Lord has done for us. Remembering the past not only brings meaning to the present but also helps us to look forward, so that the new thing God wants to do in our lives can be conceived in us. This new thing is often bigger and more daring than 'the consecrated risks' we have taken in the past: 'remembering old patterns can suggest fresh meanings for the future'.[13] So take time out to rest, to remember, to be quiet and to trust, so that hope can be renewed in you, for 'those who hope in the Lord will renew their strength. They will soar on wings like eagles; they will run and not grow weary, they will walk and not be faint' (Isaiah 40:31). I need that kind of energy for all that lies ahead!

Re-creation

You might want to acquire a notebook in which to record your inner journey if you intend to work through the 'Re-creation' sections of this book. Journalling in this way forms a valuable means of remembering later—especially once our grey cells begin to lose their edge. I honestly wish I'd taken time to journal over the last decade, even if it was only one entry a week.

Take some time out to reflect and remember key events in your spiritual life. It might help to take a walk to a safe, quiet place where you can be alone with God. If you feel it might be useful, try the folded A4 paper exercise as a framework for your remembering, or devise your own way of mapping your life history.

- Make a list of the ways in which God has shown you his faithfulness—and thank him.
- Are there any disappointments in your life that you need to face before you can move on? It is important to forgive the past, others and ourselves, to become free to be all the Lord wants us to be in the present and the future. If you feel you need support in this, it may be wise to seek out a Christian friend or counsellor.
- Try to use any points of pain in your past constructively: they can act as lenses through which we see the hand of God in our lives. It is not easy, but when we take time to search back through our lives and examine our souls, the work of the hand of God in our journey is revealed. He pours out his blessings through our difficult experiences, not in spite of them.

Prayer

Lord, as I look back over my life, help me to remember the ways in which you have guided me and the blessings that you have poured out upon me. Show me the ways that you have helped me to grow and change in response to your love and grace. Help me to hold firmly to my belief in your faithfulness and unfailing love, so that my capacity for hope is sustained.

For reflection

Hope begins in the dark; the stubborn hope that if you just show up and try to do the right thing, the dawn will come. You wait and watch and work: you don't give up.[14]

Chapter Two

Laughing at the days to come

She is clothed with strength and dignity;
she can laugh at the days to come.

Proverbs 31:25

I had been avoiding the issue all morning and now the afternoon was well underway. Admittedly I had to take my car for an inspection at 9 o'clock and that took an hour. However, I did not have to stop at the garden centre on the return journey, even though there was a sale and I saved a fortune by getting next year's vegetable seeds at half price. In order to redeem the time I'd whittled away looking at the plants and gardening gizmos, I chose to finish the journey home on the motorway. Bad choice. I ended up spending the next two hours slowly baking in my own sweat in stationary traffic on the M25 and only avoided more waiting by taking a detour up the M1 so that I could make a U-turn back to the town where I live. Once I was home, I had lunch, made chutney, researched the possibilities of buying a chicken coop plus feathery inmates, and checked my email before forcing myself to face up to the fact of my publishing deadline.

Besides the actual miles travelled, you could draw a lot of 'life miles' out of my morning and lunch-time escapades. There are some obvious parallels: being in such a hurry that you end up stationary in the fast lane of life, or the frustration of having to make long detours to rectify bad life-choices, simply to get back where you should have been going in the first place. The major lesson for me, though, is how we use busyness to avoid the situations that we actually need to do business with. Stuck in the traffic, I finished reading Erica James' *Tell It to the Skies*. She writes the following about her main character, victim of abuse by an over-zealous, religiously motivated relative: 'Keeping relentlessly busy was the answer, she'd found. Leave herself with no time to dwell on those old memories and she was able to put it out of her mind.'[1]

Perhaps you feel the same in relation to the challenge to stop and review your past. We all have some painful issues stashed away that we'd rather not revisit, but tracing back over our lives gives us an opportunity to settle up old accounts and find a measure of healing so that we can move forward as more complete beings.[2] Once we have done that, we are in a position to take stock of the present, by which I mean the period of life in which we find ourselves now, rather than the 'present moment' that I encouraged readers to appreciate in *Barefoot in the Kitchen*. I dealt with my most painful memories of the past about 16 years ago, so, thankfully, I don't need a complete overhaul, just an occasional review. Nonetheless, I must admit that leaving the situation of being 'married' to parish ministry for 25 years gave me more baggage to unpack than I had anticipated.[3] Sorting through those issues has been somewhat entwined with the challenges of 'facing up to 50', and has taken the best part of the two years we have been out of the vicarage. Yet I hope that dealing with that aspect of my experience has left me in a position take a good look at my life as it stands now.

When I think about taking stock of the present, my thoughts always go to two Old Testament widows: the widow at Zarephath (1 Kings 17:7–24) and the widow with the jars of oil (2 Kings 4:1–7). Both were women who had experienced a drastic change in their circumstances—in both cases, due to the loss of a husband, subsequent loss of income, and debt. Each woman was in a different stage of dealing with grief, both were challenged by a man of God to take stock of their situation, both were encouraged to act, and both had their lives and family circumstances changed for the better when they did act. In the past, these stories have helped me to focus on what I have at hand and to make the most of what I have by placing it in God's hands. Over the last couple of years, that focus has changed for me. I can now see that, to get to the point of being able to take stock, those two women first had to work through their grief.

The inner journey that many women take when they are facing up to the second half of life is, in some ways, similiar to the journey made by those in the throes of grief. Think about it: at this stage of life, we 'lose' a lot, and there is nothing we can do about it. If we have given the last decade or so to bringing up children who have now left home, we may feel as if we have lost not just our children but also our sense of purpose. The gap they leave in our lives opens up the time to dwell on the thought that the best opportunities in life may have gone by, especially those to do with career. We may feel that there is no time to catch up with the more enlightened of our sisters who were working mothers from the start. We may have other regrets that suddenly loom disproportionately at the front of our minds, particularly the realisation that we are ageing. Watching youth receding rapidly as we rack up successive birthdays can be difficult to cope with, particularly if we struggle with our weight and are concerned about our body image. Losing stamina is another issue. Our bodies may no longer be up to gardening all day or wallpapering into the early hours of the morning. One thing we may be glad to see the back of is the monthly period, but even that can precipitate a sense of loss, confirming as it does that our childbearing days are gone for ever. Dealing with—or even avoiding dealing with—all these losses is hard work, especially when we struggle with self-worth and a lack of purpose. Sadly, for some, this struggle can trigger various degrees of depression.

Facing up to the second half of life involves the various stages of grief—all of which I have experienced in some form or another:

- Shock
- Denial
- Depression
- Anger
- Acceptance

The shock of the fact that I was entering midlife first hit me when I was finishing my PhD. There were two grant-giving bodies to which I could apply for funding for post-doctoral research, but, on reading the small print, I saw that one of them would not take applications from anyone over 35 years of age. I was 47. I did not feel old. My brain had not yet started dangling words or concepts tantalisingly beyond my mental grasp, and I felt that I was on the verge of getting a well-earned second chance at an academic career. After the second grant-giving body turned me down during the last round of selection, I did the maths and realised I would be 50 by the time the next round of applications was complete. I needed to face the inevitable and reinvent myself again in terms of my working life: there was no time to go though the grant application process once more, only to be turned down yet again.

Denial kicked in when I tried to find a job in the real world. Despite all my qualifications (my children joke that I have the same number of degrees as a well-known American female vocal group), along with my years of life experience and accumulated transferable skills, I was just not as employable as a bright young 20-something. I tried for a position on a management programme with a multinational company famous for its flatpack furniture, only to be offered a position selling hotdogs in their flagship store. Eventually I ended up as a part-time administrator in a college, in order to get some experience working with databases so that I could perhaps get a better job later. The place where I worked seemed to be staffed mainly by middle-aged women. Despite falling into the same age category, I was in total denial of the idea that I was 'like that'. I recently felt that denial again when I attended our oldest son's graduation. The auditorium was full of greying parents, and it was a shock to realise that my days of being a young mum among young mums were over. Our children have grown up—and we have grown older.

While I would not say that I have been depressed about entering the second half of life, I have certainly had my wistful moments. On one occasion, I found myself alone in the house on a Saturday night when my husband was away and all the children out partying with their friends. Feeling somewhat left out, I resorted to a romantic comedy on DVD, a glass of wine and a bar of chocolate, and snuggled up with the cat on my lap. While this might be a bit of a 'woman alone' cliché, I was able to laugh at myself and it actually cheered me up. True depression is quite different. It involves a protracted sense of despondency and desperation that can seem impossible to shake off, an emptiness in which no apparent comfort can be found. I remember feeling that way when I suffered with post-natal depression. Whereas I find that moments of wistfulness can usually be cured by purposeful activity rather than allowing myself to sit and sink into a pool of self-pity, true depression cannot be shaken off so easily. The way out of depression can be a long and lonely road, although, in my case, when the time came I was 'snapped out of it' by healing prayer and the practical support of a good friend.

As far as anger is concerned, I must admit, there have been times when I've cried because of the changes coming over me. I don't want to be what I consider 'fat'; I don't want my skin to start getting that texture I used to find so intriguing on the faces of older people; I don't want the hairs on my legs to start sprouting out of my chin; I don't want to have to wear flat shoes; I don't want to be put on the scrapheap at work; I don't want to have to get my glasses out to read food labels in supermarkets; I don't want to look a fool when I forget my PIN number at checkouts and have panic attacks in car parks because I can't for the life of me remember where I left my car. I know I can't stop it happening: the signs are all there, and tears have been an important part of the process of letting go. While these issues may not sound like much to some people, they matter a lot to me because I want to stay the way I have been for the last few decades. I don't want my physical and mental attributes to deteriorate. For others, the issues may be greater: women I know have had to struggle with redundancy, life-threatening illness, desertion by their spouse and major problems with ailing parents and errant children. These things can hit you just when you hope that life should start to open up, cut you some slack and provide some 'me time'. No wonder midlife women experience anger.

The last stage of grief is acceptance. I've heard it said that drowning is quite a pleasant experience once you stop struggling. While that is rather a negative analogy, there are some parallels with the second half of life. I have pretty much managed to stop struggling and have begun to find a strange kind of acceptance of what is happening. As the American comedian Anita Renfroe says in 'Wrinkled Ladies' (her parody of Beyoncé's raunchy pop video 'Single Ladies'), 'You can't hide it so you gotta make peace with it'![4] At the same time, acceptance does not mean giving up and giving in. Acceptance is about facing up to the reality of a situation and resolving to make the best of it. As they say, 'If life throws you lemons, make lemonade'—and women do. If you look around, you can see 'women of all backgrounds essentially opening up the Great Midlife Lemonade Stand, taking the bitter taste out of ageing and making it sweet and satisfying'.[5]

Acceptance, then, is a place of peace where we can dry our tears and take the opportunity to look at all the pieces of our lives and imagine the variety of patterns we can make by rearranging them. This is very similar to the place where I found myself during the writing of *Barefoot in the Kitchen*. The barefoot exercise—taking off my shoes in my kitchen and feeling the cold floor under my feet—was an intentional way of bringing myself down to size, helping myself get in touch with reality and finding my natural stance. Perhaps, in some ways, life has travelled in a circle, as, during the really hot weather of the last few weeks of term, I prised off my high-heeled slingbacks under my desk at work. Unwilling to put them back on to go and talk to a colleague at the next bank of desks, I wandered across the office barefoot. While it was not quite 'barefoot in the boardroom', the symbolism was not lost on me after my three years of struggle to settle down in that organisation. My job isn't high-powered, and taking my shoes off was a timely reminder to me to stay humble in the face of reality and not to think more highly of myself than I ought.

Going back to the two widows I mentioned earlier, the woman in Zarephath had definitely reached an acceptance of her situation. However, her form of acceptance was akin to negative resignation. She could see no way out and had made up her own mind that her life and the life of her son were over. When asked by Elijah for a drink of water and some bread, she replied, 'As surely as the Lord your God lives, I don't have any bread—only a handful of flour in a jar and a little oil in a jug. I am gathering a few sticks to take home and make a meal for myself and my son, that we may eat it—and die' (1 Kings 17:12). What I find fascinating is that the Lord had previously said to Elijah, 'Go at once to Zarephath of Sidon and stay there. I have commanded a widow in that place to supply you with food' (v. 9). By the looks of things, the widow knew that Elijah was coming, she had received a recognisable command from God, but she had decided in her own heart that she didn't even have enough for her own needs, never mind those of a stranger.

Midlife can bring many kinds of challenge and crisis, tragedy and disappointment across our path—including redundancy, ill health, divorce, bereavement or homelessness—but, in the midst of our struggles, I believe we ignore the 'command of the Lord' for us at our peril. As I have said before, the Lord knows the plans he has for us, plans for a future and a hope (Jeremiah 29:11), so there must be an up-side that can be found through and after the worst situations. Extremes aside, the temptation to throw our hands in the air and slide into indifference and pure self-preservation is also there. We always have a choice, even if it is just the choice of our attitude and perspective on life.

The widow in Zarephath had more than she realised—a son, a house and some food—and she had not counted on God's supernatural intervention through the prophet Elijah.

Her circumstances turned round in an instant, once she responded to Elijah's request and heeded his instruction not to be afraid (v. 13). Fear is an emotion that can so often hold us back in midlife. Our minds are full of the 'what-ifs'. When my husband first tabled the notion that we could have a life outside parish ministry, all I could see were the 'what-ifs'. I was terrified. I did not want to put the little we'd got into such a risky God-project and tried to resolve my fear by reading all sorts of self-help books on facing uncertainty. No one says you have to throw away your brain and ignore the risks but, in the end, the best you can do is to take an informed, calculated risk and trust God for the rest. And was it as bad as I thought? No. The worst that has happened is the episode of pouring water through the kitchen ceiling of our first 'real' home. The plumber has been; the loss adjuster is coming, and so is the builder-decorator. Looking on the up-side, it has been a wonderful learning experience: now I know that we can deal with emergencies on our own without the back-up of the Diocesan Estates Management team. Besides, I get two new ceilings courtesy of my insurance company, both of which needed attention before the flood, and the patience I seem to have acquired in midlife has taken a lot of the stress out of the whole process.

The widow in 2 Kings 4 showed a different kind of acceptance than the widow in Zarephath. She had lost a husband, and her sons were about to be sold into slavery to pay his debts, but she was not resigned. She had taken stock of the situation but was still angry. She cried out to Elisha the prophet in a 'What are you going to do about it?' tone of voice that contained a hint of blame. Perhaps he had overseen the school of prophets that her husband had belonged to, and she felt he had some responsibility to help her. Like so many of us when we face difficulty, maybe she was hoping he would dig his hands into his pockets and bail her out with the equivalent of a material gift. Elijah did help her, but not in the way she expected. He said to her, 'Tell me, what do you have in your house?' (v. 2). At this point, we see that she did have an element of resignation about the situation, just like the other widow. She replied, 'Your servant has nothing there at all, except a little oil.' You can almost hear her adding, 'And what use do you expect that to be? I haven't got anything to cook in the oil, have I?'

I would venture to describe such a reaction as sadly typical of so many women. We all tend to play down what we have, thinking it is insufficient, not good enough, not worth anything, or not much use. If I had a pound for every time I've heard myself say something similar, never mind all the times I've heard other women saying it, I'd be very rich indeed.

The positive side of the widow's attitude, though, was that she refused to take the situation lying down. An element of anger—positive anger, not bitter anger—is often needed to provide the drive that spurs us into action, so we need not park all such emotion, in the search for acceptance. Just as forgiveness does not involve denying that a painful situation ever happened, acceptance does not mean that we have to sit still and let a situation remain the same. In 1 Corinthians 7:21, Paul asks, 'Were you a slave when you were called? Don't let it trouble you—although if you can gain your freedom, do so.' This says to me that although some things cannot be changed and we may need to learn to accept them with all due humility, if a situation is unsatisfactory and can be changed, then we have an opportunity to take action that will make a difference.

On the negative side, the widow was looking to blame someone else for her misfortune, looking to someone else to sort it out, and could not see the potential of what she already had in her possession if God was allowed into the equation. She did not just have a little oil; she had her health and resolve, organising capabilities, some jars and containers, two sons to help her, a network of helpful neighbours and a local outlet where she could sell merchandise. Looking at the wider situation showed her that there were more pieces to be put into the equation and thus more possibilities than she had realised. When she poured the oil into the jars she had and the jars she managed to borrow, it did not stop flowing until there were no more jars left. I am sure her sons helped her carry the jars to market and return them to the neighbours once she had sold the goods to her customers.

Years ago, when my children were still small, I needed some extra cash. I looked at what I'd got and it did not seem much—a vegetable garden full of lettuce and herbs. Standing back and looking at the wider picture, though, I decided to take a risk. I cut the lettuces and herbs, washed them, spun them dry, put them in clean polythene bags and sold them locally as organic, ready-washed herb salad, undercutting some of the larger supermarkets. I'm not sure the health and safety laws would let me do the same now, but in two previous homes I have managed to get environmental health certificates for my kitchen so that I can cook foodstuffs for sale at local craft fairs. At about the same time as the salad enterprise, I wrote a letter in response to an article in a Christian magazine. The editor printed the letter and then rang me up and asked if I wanted to take over the column— which I did for two years. That was the beginning of what one of my office colleagues calls a 'successful writing career', although it's not so successful that I could give up the day job to pursue it. Nevertheless, both ventures could have been taken to greater levels if I had pushed them. The lesson for us is not to despise 'the day of small things' (Zechariah 4:10).

So how do you take stock of your life? Like reviewing your past, taking stock requires time and space to get away, and probably a notebook and pen. Having said that, some of my best thinking is done while performing routine domestic tasks—chopping vegetables, washing up, folding laundry, vacuuming, sweeping the kitchen floor, weeding, or mowing the lawn. The repetitiveness of the task stills the mind and gives it time to meditate on all that's going on in the subconscious. The key is not to do these jobs to music: an element of silence is needed. If the TV is on in the sitting-room, close the kitchen door. Rather like learning to meditate, beginning to take stock needs time. It can't be done within one washing-up session or one walk to work, but takes place over a period of time in which these reflections are performed. Then comes the 'a-ha!' moment when it is time to sit down, grab your notebook and write everything down before you forget what the flash of clarity actually was.

To make the thinking easier, I tend to break my life down into areas and think about each one as the need takes me: home and family, work, me, church, and friends. Obviously some of the areas include quite a lot of issues that need to be weighed one at a time—issues that can change overnight for families in relation to the antics of older children, ageing parents and an unpredictable job market.

'Home and family' includes my husband and his concerns, my children and their individual concerns, the concerns of our wider family, especially older relatives, maintaining the fabric of our home, and routine domestic demands—including the needs of our pets, mortgage payments and looking after the upkeep of my burgeoning suburban smallholding. The list goes on, and in there somewhere are my own personal concerns, especially the constant fight against clutter to preserve the order and simplicity I find so essential to maintaining my inner peace.

'Work' presents various issues, particularly the need to balance the tasks I would like to take on with the demands in other areas of my life. 'Church' is a tricky issue for me at the moment. No longer a vicar's wife, I am not ready to assume any level of commitment in a local church, although I have come to a point where I have begun to feel part of the fellowship I attend. I am enjoying the chance to rest, to recover after years of active involvement, and find myself, but the time is coming when some decisions will have to be made about the extent to which I become actively involved in this community.

'Me' tends to be the biggest issue for most of us, and I am no exception. As I sat waiting for my car to be serviced yesterday, I listed the following areas of the 'Me' part of my life that I may need to look at afresh: contentment, fulfilment, self-image, self-discipline, security and health. I'm sure there are more. Some of these issues are based on outer needs but they all have a bearing on deeper inner needs, too. It is those inner needs that often require attention at midlife, when so much redefining of identity must occur. Our attitudes and commitment to family, friends, work and church will necessarily flow from the conclusions we reach from such self-scrutiny, if we are to find any authenticity in the way we tackle the second half of life. We need to work from the inside out rather than the outside in—unlike those companies that will sell us any number of midlife fixes, from oil of evening primrose tablets to plastic surgery.

We must evaluate our 'sense of connection' to ourselves, to others and to God, and 'the corresponding emotions that intertwine to create the unique response of each woman to her midlife experience'.[6] In the remaining three chapters of this book, I am going to reflect on the areas of 'Me', 'Home and family' and 'Work' in an attempt to help us identify what we 'have in our house' and how we can use it in the years ahead of us. As I don't believe that God can be put in a box, each chapter will touch on how our faith has a bearing on the area of life under discussion. I'm very much aware that my life experience is different from that of other women and my share of tragedy has probably been less than for some, but it can help to know that we all ask similar questions and struggle with similar dilemmas. Once we have allowed the Holy Spirit to do the necessary work in our hearts, I hope we will be ready and able to 'laugh at the days to come' (Proverbs 31:25).

Re-creation

Are you:
- always on the look-out for signs of ageing?
- harbouring regrets?
- believing that the greatest life opportunities are behind you?
- sensing a lack of purpose?
- regarding your life to date as somewhat disappointing?
- seeing the future in a negative light?

If so, then according to Dr Miriam Stoppard, there is the possibility that you are in the throes of a midlife crisis.[7] Don't reach for your usual comforter, whether that's a bar of chocolate, a glass of red wine or your credit card. Instead, resolve to let the Holy Spirit help you start the inner work of the heart that eventually leads to active acceptance.

- Take some time out to reflect on whether you have begun a process of grieving as youth recedes into the past. If so, what stage of the grieving process do you think you have reached? What events and feelings do you associate with the stages of grief you may have already passed through?
- Write down the specific things that cause you to fret when you think about the second half of life. Consciously put them into the Lord's hands in prayer: 'Cast all your anxiety on him because he cares for you' (1 Peter 5:7).
- Cultivate a gratitude attitude! This is a good way to start taking stock and looking at your life in the present. It is a documented medical fact that people who regularly count their blessings in the context of a life of faith live longer and enjoy better health.[8] Perhaps keep a notebook by your bed and write down three blessings that you have received in the day that has just passed.

Prayer

Lord, in the times when I struggle to come to terms with the swift passage of years, may I know the reassuring presence of your Spirit and understand that I am still beautiful in your eyes, loved by you just as greatly as I ever was, and still have much of value and use to offer in your service.

For reflection

If you've never cried hard, you can never laugh hard. The inner depth that gets opened up by the sadness can also be filled with joy much greater. Joy is the evidence of the presence of divinity...

There is nothing in old age that can stop you from feeling a deep and abiding joy, except your own attitude. When you're old, your attitude is still the great freedom left to you.[9]

By the time we hit fifty, we have learned our hardest lessons. We have found out that only a few things are really important. We have learned to take life seriously, but never ourselves.[10]

Chapter Three

Anxious thoughts and offensive ways

Search me, O God, and know my heart;
test me and know my anxious thoughts.
See if there is any offensive way in me,
and lead me in the way everlasting.

Psalm 139:23–24

I have taken quite a while to get round to writing this chapter on taking stock of my 'self'. Spending time in preparation, by thinking about my regrets and passions, spurred me to take action and do something that I am passionate about while I am on leave from work, rather than sitting and writing about it. So I have spent the afternoon in my garden. First I planted out the front garden with the ornamental kales and cabbages I have raised from seed. They produce an array of colour, shape, texture and height right through the winter, their colours intensifying as the temperature drops. Each year I try a different pattern and, so far, we have never failed to see people stop and stare at my potager as they walk past to the shops. Then I thinned a ragged row of tangled seedlings down to 35 strong, well-spaced plants that should give a good helping of mashed winter roots for Sunday lunch, all winter. On the way back to the house, I noticed that the dried chickpeas I planted for fun from the bag in the pantry have now produced small white flowers. It is fascinating how something so small and apparently insignificant can produce such a feeling of gratification and deep satisfaction.

Now at the table in the dining-room, looking out over my garden, it's back to the work of personal stock-taking. I began the process in bed on Sunday morning with a waffle and jam and a hot mug of tea. Being a 'list person', the best way I could see of approaching the issue was to divide my life into three sections (body, mind and spirit), reflect on each section in turn, and see what might need developing in each area for the next stage of life to accomplish 'what I want'.

The expression 'what I want' does not sit easily within me, or, I suspect, with many women. Sigmund Freud said, 'The great question, which I have not been able to answer, despite my thirty years of research into the feminine soul, is "What does a woman want?"'[1] It is my belief that one of the reasons many women do not know what they want is due to generations of conditioning to put others first, which causes confusion and guilt when a woman is asked what she herself actually wants. The easiest thing to say is, 'I don't know!' because, until recently, women have not often had permission from society to admit that they want anything other than what society demands from them. Jesus' command to love others, and especially his statement that the greatest love is to lay down one's life for others (John 15:13), can intensify the tendency of too many women to push their own desires to the bottom of their list of priorities. In my experience, younger women tend to be better at prioritising their own needs, and women of more mature years could do with taking a leaf out of their book. After all, it was the brave and radical women of our generation who wrote that book for them in the first place, by standing up for women's rights so that emerging generations can enjoy the freedoms they sometimes so easily take for granted.

I admit that I am not much good at prioritising my needs. I have spent ten days of my 16 days' leave running around after other members of the family in the hope that, once their needs are satisfied, there will be some time left for me. After nearly 27 years of marriage and 22 years of child-raising, you'd have thought I'd know by now that that is unlikely to happen. I've watched everyone else get on with what they wanted and thought, 'Hey, why should things be any different for me?' At midlife, it is so important that women ask themselves what they want and what they need, in order to make the second half of life happy, healthy and fulfilling. Ultimately, the responsibility is ours, and it is natural that we start to ask ourselves such questions: 'As we age, we see ourselves as less sensitive and less controlled by other people's demands and expectations. We are less interested in relationships that are obligatory rather than reciprocal. The direction of change is toward tending to ourselves… we learn what we want when we recall our voices, half buried under other people's wants and needs, and bring those values and ideas to light.'[2]

The biblical command that would be a better focus for midlife women is 'to love your neighbour as your self' (Matthew 22:39)—with an emphasis on the requirement to love your *self*. For too many women, loving their neighbour as much as they presently love themselves would mean displaying a very poor love. Speaking personally, loving my self is not something that comes naturally to me, so a stock-take based on body, mind and spirit—working from the outside in, so that I can live from the inside out—was bound to be interesting. I share some of my thoughts with you in the hope that they will prompt your own self-inventory and resolution.

Body

Ever since I started having children, I have struggled with my body image. Looking at photos from those days, I realise now that I had nothing to worry about then. After my breakfast of a waffle and tea this morning, I dug out the scales and dared to weigh myself. Not good news. I've put on an extra pound a month since the beginning of the year and am nearly as heavy as I was during my fourth pregnancy. Action is urgently required, but I worry that a 'diet' approach dooms me to failure. It's better to go for a radical readjustment of my eating habits and keep in mind the calorie limit for my particular body mass index, especially as I have a sedentary full-time job. Our metabolism slows down as we get older and we don't need to eat so much, so what I eat needs to be healthy and (given my family's predisposition to strokes) low in cholesterol. I need to stop cooking for six when only three usually show up, especially as the temptation to have a second helping is exacerbated by my waste-not-want-not mentality. I should not nibble while I'm cooking, only to eat again when the meal is cooked. I must stop taking cakes to work for my colleagues and snacking on them myself, leave my purse at home so that I'm not tempted by workplace vending machines and say 'No' to all the goodies brought into the office after high days and holidays.

Alcohol is another issue for me. I am not happy to admit that the stress of vicarage life, the generosity of our church members and my own weak will led me to consume more red wine in an average week than was good for me during the last few years as a vicar's wife. I want to get back to the way things were when my husband was a curate: one low-budget bottle for Friday night because it was all we could afford. That makes it more special—and a *little* bit of red wine is stuffed full of healthy anti-oxidants.

Thinking 'body' also means thinking 'health'. I'm surprised the neighbours can't hear me rattling down the street because of the number of supplements I take in the morning: calcium and vitamin D for bones, cod liver oil for my joints, senna for my gut, and a vitamin B complex for everything else. I have also realised that it is a priority to keep up my own dental visits now that I am no longer taking the children, and to ensure I have regular eye checks now that I am using a computer at work all day long. I've also found that a low-maintenance body has suddenly become high-maintenance: visits to the hairdresser and pedicures used to be a luxury, but now I need to go more often to keep hair in place and stop painful cracks from appearing in my heels. My daughter has also decided to introduce me to the joys of waxing—not legs, mind you, but my chin!

What about moving that body? Exercise is good for everyone, including midlife women, as it causes the cells in our bodies to release natural chemicals called endorphins that help us feel good about ourselves, as well as keeping various parts of our bodies working efficiently for longer. I have never joined a gym as I resent exercising for no end other than fitness. Instead, I have always done exercise with a byproduct, like raking up leaves, vacuuming the house, digging the vegetable patch, traipsing upstairs and down-stairs with piles of clean laundry, bending up and down to hang wet washing, and cleaning windows—and I do cycle to work. Nevertheless, maybe I should take advantage of the state-of-the-art gym opening next month in the new college building. At least it would keep me away from the biscuit tin and out of the shops during office lunch-times.

What we put on our body, our clothes, also becomes an

issue as we reach middle age. Despite the changes we begin to experience, women still want to look good, and can do so. The main frustration comes from trying to find a style that suits the kind of life we lead, and shops that sell the type of clothes we want. Most of the high street shops seem to cater for younger women, stocking clothes that are not well made or of good quality and do not flatter the more mature female figure. I suppose this is why makeover shows on TV are so popular: there is a whole generation of older women out there who desperately need someone to show them what to wear and how to wear it. Once you have found your style (or, perhaps, different styles for different aspects of your life), it's a good idea to stick to it, or, at least, to variations on the theme. There is no boost to the self-confidence like being happy in the clothes you are in, although I like to remind myself on a regular basis that real beauty and self-confidence radiate from within. No amount of fancy clothes can hide a hurting heart or a wounded soul.

As a footnote to the physical aspect of our self-inventory, we come to footwear. Shoes have always mattered to me: I love them. That is why it was such a big deal for me to lay aside my high heels, as I described in *Barefoot in the Kitchen*. Now back at work, I have rediscovered the joy of heels—and, lately, the agony. I'm not ready to wear 'flatties' yet, but maybe it is time to find something both stylish and practical. That would get the Health and Safety Officer off my case, anyway: I think she's worried I'll break an ankle on the stairs and sue the college! In my opinion, we should enjoy such small pleasures as shoes while we can. This was recently brought home to me when a female colleague confided that she has early onset diabetes, a condition that can occur in middle-age. The doctor had prescribed special footwear because of her condition, and we both sat at my desk and rued the frumpiness of the styles in the catalogue he had given her. So my final word on 'body' would be to look after what you've got and appreciate it.

Mind

Valuing, nurturing and loving ourselves—a combination of what we know and how we feel about ourselves—is not only an essential basis for caring for our bodies inside and out; it is also important for tending our hearts and our minds. Knowledge about midlife transitions is relatively easy to come by. Information is available on the internet or in local libraries and bookshops, which is why I have not spent time detailing facts and figures and lists of menopausal symptoms. What we feel about that knowledge and how we deal with it in relation to our own situation is the valuing and nurturing debt of self-love that we owe to ourselves.

I am not a trained counsellor so I have no professional way of knowing how to get in touch with my feelings regarding midlife passage, but the verse at the head of this chapter has always provided a good starting point for me: 'Search me, O God, and know my heart; test me and know my anxious thoughts. See if there is any offensive way in me, and lead me in the way everlasting (Psalm 139:23–24). As I understand it, 'anxious thoughts' spring from a mind that is not fully focused on Christ, and 'offensive ways' spring from a heart that does not seek to walk in authenticity. By that, I mean a heart that will not, or cannot, face up to who the person really is and can become in the fullness of the purpose of God. God demands truth in our inner being (Psalm 51:6), and this means that we must learn not to be ashamed of ourselves, because he made us and longs to continue shaping us as his beloved, precious children.

My own anxious thoughts tend to centre on regrets and fears. Regrets are usually about what we have not done, as opposed to rueing what we have done. Looking back, I think I can safely say that I do not regret the choices I have made, because I can see the pattern of God's faithfulness in the chain of events that has made up my life so far. I am a firm believer in Romans 8:28: 'And we know that in all things God works for the good of those who love him, who have been called according to his purpose.' Nevertheless, identifying regrets from the past can help us address character issues that might hold us back in the future. I wondered the other day what my life would have been like now if I had cashed in my postgraduate teacher training 27 years ago and become a science teacher. I was punched in the face by a 15-year-old during one of my teaching practices, and, although I finished the course, I never taught. Why? I think I was frightened, not just of the pupils but of the demands the job might have placed on me.

Have there been other times in my life when I failed to follow through like this? Yes, I believe there have—for example, the time 20 years ago when I was asked by an American publisher to write a novel and I backed off because I was afraid I would not be able to produce what they wanted. Whatever the reason, I know that I need to examine this tendency more closely if I am to make the most of the years ahead, especially now that I (theoretically) have the maturity to deal with the issue.

Fear can stunt our emotional and spiritual growth. I have to admit that I am a fearful person—my biggest fears being that something awful might happen to one of our children or that we might lose our lovely house and garden. I am still trying to get to the bottom of why I am like this, but at least I am aware of the fears in my life, especially when I am faced with new situations and challenges. Perhaps the root of all the fear is essentially a fear of failure. Being a perfectionist and very competitive, I have an overdeveloped and possibly unhealthy drive to succeed. And why am I a competitive perfectionist? I think that part of it is just the way I am made, and a large part of it is the need for approval. Why do I need so much approval? I suppose I may need to analyse my childhood and my relationship with my parents to answer that question. Yet, now I am 'older and wider', my need for approval is diminishing, and this is an enormous relief. I think that as women get older, they get beyond caring what other people think of them. For example, if I want to ride my bicycle to work wearing unsuitable shoes, then I will—and I do, every working day—despite the comments I get from friends and strangers alike. This is indeed the beginning of authenticity, of finding and being your true self.

So much for my anxious thoughts, but what about the 'offensive ways' mentioned in Psalm 139:24? By this I do not mean my tendency to utter unsuitable expletives while I'm cooking dinner and mulling over the events of the working day, although I could do with stopping that bad habit. In an attempt to identify 'offensive ways' that may need rooting out of the heart in the search for authenticity, I have found these words from Pamela Blair, an American psychotherapist, helpful: 'Some of the many gifts of the midlife passage include the death of our attempts to control and letting go of protective masks, letting go of manipulative behaviour... unrealistic self-images, unhealthy addictions, protective illusions, old gods and expectations. As older women we can choose to be authentic in all we do.'[3]

Sadly, the 25 years I spent as a vicar's wife gave me much personal experience of hiding behind protective masks and living up to expectations, and probably indulging in protective illusions and unhealthy addictions. This was nothing to do with the particular churches in which my husband served; it is an experience that I have found to be common to many (but not all) women 'married to the ministry'. Like it or not, vicar's wife is a role that suits some people better than others, and I found that it did not fit me well, although I always did my best in every situation. In this respect I took great comfort from Grace Shepherd's book, *An Aspect of Fear*, when I read it over a decade ago.[4] As a vicar's wife and subsequently a bishop's wife, she struggled with the public side of her husband's ministry. Her honesty in print helped me to understand that my struggles were real and gave me permission not be so hard on myself when I found vicarage life too much. The last two years have provided a great opportunity to learn to be myself, sometimes to the amusement of friends and colleagues. I have not done much conscious work during this process of healing and growth, but I've allowed the passage of time, liberally sprinkled with bouts of reflection while carving out my new vegetable garden, to gently unravel my tangled thoughts and feelings.

Reading through and correcting this manuscript several months after completing the first draft, I am encouraged to note that progress has been made. Healing, growth and self-discovery take time, and as I sat in the cold February sunshine with my husband and we reflected over the journey of the last few years, I was reminded that we all tend to overestimate what we can achieve in a year, but vastly underestimate what we can achieve in five. No matter whether the aim is the physical establishment of a suburban smallholding or the spiritual aim of allowing the Holy Spirit to do a recreative work in the soul, these things take time and we need to be kind to ourselves in the process.

Spirit

Most of the writing I have come across that touches on the spiritual side of a woman's life at middle-age is very syncretistic: it incorporates a bit of every faith going. Typically these books describe our spiritual self as an essential aspect of ourselves—'the higher self, the real self, the centre that feels like home when we connect with it'.[5] As a Christian, I would prefer to describe the spiritual part of myself as the place where I know God's presence in my life, the bit of me that communes with the Spirit of God, the place that is the seat of my relationship with him. Examining our relationship with God is no bad thing at any time of life, but at midlife this kind of review takes a new sense of urgency in the light of the overall quest for purpose and meaning.

To be honest, my personal spiritual quest over the last few years has taken me to the brink of unbelief and back. I have had the time and space to dare even to doubt God's existence and work through the possible implications for me of believing there to be no God at all. Unhappy with a glimpse into the Godless realm in which so many people choose to live, and conscious of the obvious intervention of God at so many points in my own journey, I was able not only to find 'rest' but also to 'return'. Remember the verse in the fourth square of my folded paper in Chapter 1? 'This is what the Sovereign Lord, the Holy One of Israel, says: "In repentance and rest is your salvation, in quietness and trust is your strength"' (Isaiah 30:15). In this verse, 'returning' and 'repentance' are much the same thing, because repentance is not just about being sorry for wrong attitudes, words or actions, but about taking a U-turn back to what you know to be right.

Once children begin to leave home and life theoretically becomes more uncluttered, we have time to take a serious look at our faith. Like clearing out our wardrobe, this is our chance to look at what fits and what doesn't, to see what might be salvaged from items we haven't worn for years, and to try things that we haven't had the courage to wear before. For me, it has been an opportunity to return to the kind of simple faith I had in my teens and 20s. This is not to say that I have thrown away 30 years of gathered spiritual experience and insight: that accumulation of wisdom has been of benefit in helping me know what to keep and what to put to one side. Once we have made an inventory of our spirituality, living faith remains the template that helps us organise the various parts of our lives into a new pattern that best fits the pieces available, and we ignore it at our peril.

So what have been the most precious spiritual keepsakes for me? Ultimately, the Christian faith is still, in the words of the hymn, 'the old, old story'—a story of forgiveness, grace, hope and power for daily living. These are among the most important aspects of faith for me. We can never stop too often to look back at our day, our week, the last year or even the last decade or so, and ask the Lord to examine our hearts, test our thoughts and point out what we need to confess, so that we can lay it at the foot of the cross and ask him to forgive us. Forgiveness is and always has been the key to inner healing and thus to spiritual growth. Yet confession can be painful. Looking back at my 'challenging year', there are many things I have thought, said, done and not done that make me want to curl up into a ball and hide. Thankfully, though, the foot of the cross is a safe place where we can allow the love of God gently to uncurl us and wrap us in a divine hug of forgiveness—a place where we can receive grace that enables us to start afresh with the past behind us.

'Grace' and 'hope' take me back to the second part of Isaiah 30:15: 'in quietness and trust is your strength'. After repentance and forgiveness, the ongoing experience of God's constant faithfulness gives us a sense of quietness and trust in our inner being that provides the strength to meet the challenges and opportunities of middle-age head on. Despite the fact that my physical stamina is not quite what it was, knowing the ongoing infilling of the Holy Spirit gives me the mental strength I need for daily living—and often that fuels my physical strength, as spirit, mind and body are intricately connected. Like many people before me, I lay great store in the promise that although youths may grow weary, 'those who hope in the Lord will renew their strength. They will soar on wings like eagles; they will run and not grow weary, they will walk and not be faint' (Isaiah 40:31).

One benefit I have found in my spiritual re-emergence has been the growing desire to return to a personal devotional time after years of praying on the run, as I've dashed around packing lunches, ironing uniforms, chauffeuring children, supervising homework and the plethora of other chores that led to the kind of spiritual scramble (as opposed to a spiritual 'walk') I described in *Barefoot in the Kitchen*. I take this as a welcome sign of long overdue spiritual maturity—maturity being indicated by doing something not because you have to but because you want to, especially when you have the time to do so and busyness is no longer a valid excuse for not stopping to be quiet in God's presence. It is not easy to describe the sense of freedom that accompanies this kind of spiritual authenticity, but it is well worth having.

Although there is nowhere we can go where we are lost to God's Spirit ('If I go up to the heavens you are there; if I make my bed in the depths, you are there', Psalm 139:8), faith provides us with more benefits if it is a shared experience as opposed to a solitary one.[6] Joining others to worship God is good for our spiritual and physical health. I mentioned earlier that finding a place in spiritual community has been a challenge for me. When my husband left parish ministry, I sought a church where I am not immediately recognised as the wife of a well-known Christian speaker, as I want to be welcomed into fellowship for who I am rather than who I am married to. I have found that need satisfied in a small Pentecostal church in the town where I live and was welcomed into full membership last autumn. It is wonderful to be part of a growing, caring, multinational community that is starting out in a new building and exploring the basics of the Christian life.

Although my reasons for finding a church of my own are probably different from those of the majority of midlife women, research shows that growing numbers of women between the ages of 45 and 64 are returning to church or beginning to attend church for the first time—across all denominations.[7] This is contrary to the decrease in numbers of younger women attending church. I believe that this numerical trend reflects not only the increased freedom from weekend family commitments that women may find as their children grow older, but also, and more importantly, women's deepening spiritual search in their middle years. Although we are all different and likely to find our spiritual home in a variety of spiritual traditions, our stories are all the same in that belonging to a church family gives us the opportunity to deepen our spiritual walk and build meaningful relationships with our fellow travellers.

Kathleen Fischer, in her book *Moving On: A spiritual journey for women of maturity*, states that 'the second half of a woman's life offers some of the most complex and spiritually rich decades she will know',[8] and in this chapter I have only been able to begin to tease out some of the threads that make up this rich tapestry. All being well, the decline we may have begun to experience in our physical and mental capacities can be balanced by a mounting hope inspired by the new horizons opening out to us. In this balancing act lies the mystery of the gospel, the holding together of 'suffering and loss with the truth of resurrection and new life'.[9] Within this tension there is much exploring to be done, and the second half of life provides a unique opportunity for us to do just this.

Re-creation

- Reflect on all the care you provide for the other people in your life. Are there areas where you could pull back in order to take more care of yourself? Think what it means for you to 'love your neighbour as your *self*'. If you gave others the sort of care you give your self, would they be better or worse off? Use your answer to help you look at ways you can love, value and nurture all aspects of your self—body, mind and spirit.
- Take some time to look your big fears in the eye. Ask yourself why the issues you have identified cause you to fear. Begin to probe more deeply and investigate whether your fears have a common underlying thread. Perhaps there is an aspect of your personality that you need to address in order to have a fuller life and make better choices in the years ahead.
- Imagine you are on your deathbed, looking back over your life. What are the things you would regret most? If your regrets mean that you need to ask for God's forgiveness, bring them to the cross one by one and leave them there.

Maybe there are people you need to forgive? Is there any action you need to take, to remedy your regrets?

- Be brave and ask yourself the million-dollar question: What do you want from the rest of your life? Within the boundaries of moral and ethical reality, is there anything you can do with what you've got, to make it happen?

Prayer

Lord, I may not like what I see in the mirror, but help me to see what changes I should make to allow me to love myself properly. I give you my grief, my regrets and my fears. Thank you for forgiving all my previous foolishness. Help me to rest in the knowledge of your unchanging love and teach me to walk the path of authenticity—to be the person you always intended me to be.

For reflection

If you're a woman there's always a good reason to put yourself last… I sometimes feel that sacrifice is written into our genes. It sits right next to the Guilt Chromosome that we inherited from our mothers.[10]

Often people attempt to live their lives backwards; they try to have more things, or more money, in order to do more of what they want, so they will be happier. The way it actually works is the reverse. You must first be who you really are, then do what you need to do, in order to have what you want.[11]

— Chapter Four —

The panini generation

'Praise be to the Lord, who this day has not left you
without a kinsman-redeemer… He will renew your life
and sustain you in your old age.'

Ruth 4:14–15

I recently mentioned to a colleague of similar vintage to myself that we were part of the proverbial 'sandwich genera-tion'—that group of women who are squashed between the demands of ageing parents and so-called grown-up, but in some ways no less troublesome, children. 'Sandwich?' she exclaimed. 'More like panini! Not just squashed, but toasted into the bargain!' I think she's right. The panini (which some would simply consider a fancy toasted sandwich) is a more fitting image for those of us who are not only being slowly melted in demanding family situations but are also trying to find their way again in the fast-paced world of the contemporary workplace.

Recently I realised that my 'meltdown' process had begun. Last summer, my father, 'deserted' by my stepmother (who was on a perfectly valid spree to Nova Scotia to trace her family history), rang me nearly every day for a fortnight complaining of nervous breakdowns and potential strokes. He lived in the south of France, so popping to his house to check he was all right was not a simple matter. When his wife returned home, I did not hear a word from him in three weeks: the only reply to my anxious calls across the Channel was an incomprehensible message on his French answerphone. Our children provide the other half of the panini hotplate, what with traffic accidents, Saturday night brushes with the police, lost valuables, broken iPods, multiple redundancies, broken romances or no romances, flooding the bathroom, and moving in and out of our new home with more regularity than a jack-in-the-box.

Where does this leave me? I am the melted cheese somewhere in the middle of the bread roll. I recall one week before my father's death when I was squashed between phone calls from my mother-in-law and my father on one hand and the many and various demands of my grown-up children on the other. I ended up taking a day off work with a raging migraine. Lying motionless on my bed in a darkened room, drugged up with anti-inflammatory tablets and practising various relaxation techniques to distance the pain, I had the opportunity to think the situation through. I came to the conclusion that the practicalities of caring for ageing parents and older children are demanding and draining, but they can be managed if a mixture of firmness and detachment is practised, a balance between finding an efficient and effective solution and maintaining a degree of self-preservation. I realised that the stress points for me are caused by my underlying desire to be the solution to everyone else's problems and to be everything to those special people that I think they want me to be. In the search for my true self in midlife, I have to learn to say that I can *do* so much but no more, and *be* so much but no more. I think I am getting there.

When my daughter came home and announced that her next money-spinning plan was to design clothes, hire a seamstress to make them up, and then sell them on her own website, I was able to listen but also able to admit out loud that I was unable to do much to help her. My life is too full and I have no more to give—financially (I have no savings to loan), practically (no, she can't have my sewing machine because, like most things our children borrow, I'll probably never see it again), spatially (where does she think she is going to store all this stuff?), physically (I am at maximum capacity with my own paid employment and extra projects), or emotionally (I haven't the energy to think how to advise her about such a risky, high-investment venture). Part of the path to authenticity is to be realistic—knowing who you are and what you can contribute, but also knowing where you have to draw the line.

Practicalities aside, I need to deal with the hidden expectations placed on me by others and myself. Somewhere in the middle of the panini, on top of the melted cheese that is my life, are the chopped red onions that are my parents' (or, to be more precise, my father's) unfulfilled dreams for my life. To be honest, I am not quite sure what those dreams were; I only know that I have a nagging sense of not having made quite as much of the opportunities my expensive education should have provided, or of not being as happy / successful / rich / fulfilled (delete as appropriate) as he might have hoped. Yet, as we get older, there comes a point when it is time to decide whether we like chopped red onions or not, and then either bite down hard and enjoy the taste or stop and pick the bits out of the cheese. Essentially, it's about making the decision to be ourselves and do what we can do to create the kind of relationship we want with our parents as we age and as they age—a relationship characterised by a new sense of acceptance and understanding, preferably from both sides.

When I started writing this chapter, my father was still alive, and I made the decision to visit France and make peace with him over a few issues while there was still time.

Midway through the writing, he was admitted to hospital in Angoulême. I did visit France in October, as intended, but my father had gone downhill more rapidly than anyone could have anticipated and I arrived too late. Seeing him in the chapel of rest was not an easy experience. I was aware of so many words unspoken, so many issues unresolved. But then I wondered if my need for resolution had not been rather selfish—a need to justify myself over the course my life has taken, compared to what he might have desired—because I cannot go back and change the past, and nor can I wave a magic wand and create a very different future. Perhaps a visit to talk at that level would have caused more harm than good. At least I had told him on the phone that I loved him.

Grief affects us all in different ways. Strange as it may seem, I was curiously happy that I was so sad at my father's death. I had worried in the past that when the time came I would find myself relieved to be rid of the nagging pressure to be something I wasn't, a pressure that was constantly at the back of my mind. My tears told me that I had indeed loved him, even though our relationship had not been everything I would have liked it to be. Taking time out to think while waiting for the funeral in France—digging my stepmother's garden—I came to the conclusion that much of the difficulty between my father and me had probably been my fault. In a pattern that has become unnervingly familiar in my life, I had shifted blame for problems in the relationship on to the other party, assuming that they had unrealistic expectations of me. In fact, every time, I was the one with the unrealistic expectations of myself, but I was too close to the issue to see it.

In the midst of my thoughts came the realisation that my father had been an extraordinary man and lived an extra-ordinary life, and, despite missing the opportunity to own his own farm or run a garden centre business, he had done the best he could with what he had got. I wondered if his missed opportunities had coloured his view of my missed opportunities, and thus formed the basis of his hopes for me? We all want our children to grab with both hands and take advantage of whatever we let pass, whether that was due to hesitation, bad choices, unfortunate circumstances, or, dare I say it, bad luck. (We live in a fallen world and inexplicably bad things do happen to good people.)

Talking frankly to my stepmother during that week in France, I managed to ask her what my father had wanted for me—those hopes (always unspoken) that had hung between us for so many years. She told me that he had wanted me to be an academic. Her answer was so simple, but it was a relief and a release. I had done everything I could to be an academic, but it had just not worked out. Perhaps some misinformed choices and bad timings were partly to blame, but not everyone with a PhD becomes a university lecturer, even if that is their ultimate dream. In the week or so after his death, I found I was able to put the burden down. Now that my father is no longer here, I have made my peace with his unfulfilled hopes for me and I can put the whole thing to bed, move on and be what I am intended to be in the next stage of my life.

Another aspect of losing parents in midlife that I had not expected to hit me so hard was the sense of being orphaned, despite the fact that I am supposed to be a grown-up. My panini-generation friend mentioned at work that losing your second parent is acknowledged to be a very difficult thing. My mother died over 20 years ago, and I did not see my father much, so I was surprised at how bereft I felt as a result of his death. I could only describe it as feeling like a boat, at first tethered at both ends, that had slipped one mooring and swung out into the stream and has now slipped the other mooring and been swept right out into the current. Despite having a loving spouse and four wonderful children, the death of my second parent left me with a sense of aloneness that was quite unexpected. In that situation, you are now the grown-up that others turn to, there is nothing between you and eternity, the years that are left suddenly seem to shrink, and you feel tired and old. Well, I can only say that this is how I have felt.

A week or so after my father died, I managed to get back to church and was overwhelmed by the comfort of knowing that God knew exactly how I felt, that he was 'on my case'. Psalm 139 has always meant a lot to me but now I was reading it through a very different pair of spectacles: 'You perceive my thoughts from afar. You discern my going out and my lying down; you are familiar with all my ways' (vv. 2–3). This is comforting to know when you are going through the motions of life as the result of bereavement and your thoughts are wandering down strange and unfamiliar paths. It is also an encouragement to know that the Lord promises never to leave us as orphans, but that he will come to us (John 14:18). Hanging on to this promise, I know that a degree of normality will return to life in God's due time, although the midlifer who has lost both parents never sees the world in quite the same way again. I hope the experience leaves me with a new depth of vision and a better sense of priorities and proportion. We need to know what really matters in life and what can be left by the wayside.

I may have lost a father but I still have a mother-in-law: my husband's adoptive mother. Our relationship has been tense at times during the last 30 years. After my inner revelations regarding my father, I am now wondering how much of that tension has been my fault, but I am thankful that, over the last seven years, our differences have already mellowed into a welcome sense of mutual respect. In the face of her extreme old age and our mutual, yet unspoken, acknowledgment of human mortality, issues that once seemed so important to each of us have, thankfully, slipped into proper perspective. It has dawned on me that I am now as old as she was when I first met her. I finally understand the frustrations she struggled with then—particularly in trying to maintain some sort of family routine and coping with the challenges associated with parenting children who were about to fly the nest. At the time, I thought those concerns were so petty, but now, surprisingly, I find that they are my own.

From her side, she is now old enough to see that I have weathered the test of time (I don't think either side of our family thought our marriage would last, because we married so young) and that, as she admitted recently, I have become all she once considered herself to be in respect of holding the family together. I feel honoured to have been conferred with this privileged responsibility, although the thought of it can be quite frightening. Strangely enough, this is not because I don't think I'm up to the challenge but because I am not sure it is actually necessary. My husband's brother and sister have their own families, and I don't think they need me rallying round, organising their lives for them in the same way that a matriarch of previous generations might have done. Looking after our own four children is quite enough!

When I contemplate the strange state of affairs that is part and parcel of becoming the generation 'in charge', I am drawn to the story of Naomi and Ruth and their unique relationship. Reading this story again as an almost 50-something (two weeks to go!), I understand it in a completely different way from the way I did when I was in my 20s. Back then, the devotion, commitment and sacrifice that Ruth showed in the face of her mother-in-law's distress were fuel for the youthful enthusiasm I felt, as I thought about supporting my husband in the life of parish ministry upon which he was about to embark. Now I see it for what it is—a story of the relationship between two women that grows and changes as they themselves grow, age, change and cope with the hardships life throws at them.

After the loss of her husband and sons, and living in a foreign country, Naomi is faced with no other choice than to return to her homeland (see Ruth 1:1–18). At least there she still has a house and probably a bit of land that she and her family had left behind ten years previously. We find no mention of who has been caring for her property in the family's absence, but, now that she is old, she hopes there may still be distant relations with whom she can restore a sense of community. I wonder if Naomi's overt challenge to her widowed daughters-in-law to return to their families was perhaps not as transparently honest as a surface reading might imply. Perhaps it was actually a double-bluff, intended to ensure that at least one of them stayed with her and helped her through her tough transition. Haven't you ever done something similar? Haven't you caught yourself saying, 'Oh no, you don't need to help me with such-and-such!' when in fact you mean the exact opposite, and the comment is articulated in such a way as to ensure the desired end?

Looking at the story in that light, Orpah was the sensible one who refused to be influenced by her scheming mother-in-law and chose to get on with her own life. Ruth, by contrast, was the naïve party, allowing her overactive guilty conscience to turn her into the proverbial doormat, to the possible detriment of her own future. But there again, looking at the story from Ruth's side, perhaps she had nothing to go home to. Perhaps what awaited her at her parents' home was worse than the prospect of travelling to a foreign land with a woman who might manipulate her for her own ends. Perhaps Ruth could see some gain to her own advantage in the situation. We will never know the full background to the story and the reasons why these women spoke and acted as they did, but it shows us that parent/adult–child relationships are complex, with a lot going on under the surface.

When they have settled in Bethlehem and Ruth suggests to Naomi that she might go and glean in the fields to provide the two of them with food, I can almost sense my own mental machinations in Naomi's reply. Naomi tells Ruth to 'go ahead' (2:2)—rather as I do when my children come to me with a suggestion that I think is practical and will reap a reward without too much complication. But then I begin to push them a little further with 'helpful' suggestions. Perhaps Naomi was not so different from me. We read, '*As it turned out*, [Ruth] found herself working in a field that belonged to Boaz' (v. 3). Now you're not going to tell me this was just a coincidence? There seems to me to be more than a hint of suggestion in the phrase 'As it turned out'! Naomi knew the land. She knew who all the fields belonged to. I'm sure she must have 'suggested' to Ruth which would be the most 'profitable' ones to glean, in more senses than one. This is rather like me, when I point one of my children in the direction of a job and then, once they are employed, drop hints that a certain course of action within that role might be to 'their' benefit. What I really mean is that a pay rise or a permanent contract will allow me the opportunity to ask for a larger contribution to the utilities bill, or might even increase the possibility of their being able to move out. I am looking after their interest, but also looking after my own!

We all know how the story ends. After some complicated manoeuvres, again orchestrated by Naomi, Ruth marries

Boaz, and Naomi gets the shelter and provision she needs in her old age—with the added bonus of a grandson to brighten her days and give her status in the community. If we put ourselves in Ruth's shoes, we see the pressure of expectations coming from the older generation. If we put ourselves in Naomi's shoes, we can identify with the kind of pressure that is so easy to inflict on our own children. We need to respect our elders and yet be ourselves while we still have some time and energy left to make something of our lives, but perhaps we need to see that there is more sense and truth in their suggestions than we care to admit. We need to release our children to find and fulfil their own dreams and yet be involved enough to steer them gently away from actions that seem to us to be obvious mistakes.

Although I have spent a fair bit of this chapter talking about relationships with the older generation, I do need to say something about the complicated nature of dealings with adult children. My children are still young adults, so I do not yet have the issues that could come with gaining a son-in-law or several daughters-in-law, plus a flock of grandchildren. Comments on that topic will need to wait for a book on facing retirement! Nevertheless, parenting young adults has its challenges. At this stage, children are old enough to look after themselves (theoretically) but they still need to know that they have caring parents and the security of a family home to fall back on when needed.

My most recent trauma concerned our oldest son, who was preparing to spend five months in Uganda doing voluntary work. I had deliberately stood back and let him take the responsibility of sorting everything out—not unreasonable, given that he is 22. All was well until 36 hours prior to his departure. I received a call at work to say that his laptop had totally crashed, and what was he to do, as he needed one to take with him. Being in the middle of a meeting, and not having a laptop of my own to offer, I had no choice but to tell him he had two hours to find what he wanted online. As I was off work that afternoon, we would go straight to the store and collect it so that he still had a day to set it up before leaving. So we did—and the bill now sits on my credit card statement until he gets back from Africa!

As I have mentioned before, I am learning where to draw the line, but it is important to me that our children can come to us with their needs, knowing that we will help if we can— even if all they need is a hug, a listening ear and a shoulder to cry on. This is despite the fact that some of them have chosen not to make our faith their own, which can complicate issues for us when we are asked for advice. Nevertheless, I believe the important thing is that the lines of communication, and the door to the family home, are kept open.

When it comes to relationships, midlife can also be a time of redefinition for our friendships and for our relationship with our spouse. Friendships have been a big issue for me, mainly because we have moved away from the village that had been our home for twelve years. These were years when our children went through primary and secondary schools, so we knew a lot of people not just through the church but also in the community. Moving to a new area, but not so far away that we could not stay in contact with some of our friends, presented an interesting dynamic. Of course it is impossible to maintain a friendship with a whole congregation when you are no longer the vicarage family, but it was a shock to my system to realise how 'alone' we suddenly felt after moving. I had recently moved office at my place of work, so I also had to adjust to a new set of immediate colleagues.

Riding the wave of midlife changes can be made so much easier by friends. I have moved house, faced changes at work and joined a new church—which has brought new neighbours, new workmates and new fellow believers. Others may have more distressing changes forced on them, such as redundancy, illness, divorce or bereavement. All such changes inevitably bring a change in our circle of friends. While some will stick with you, others will fall by the wayside, perhaps simply because your new situation does not fit their pattern of life any more.

Making and maintaining friends takes time and effort; it doesn't happen overnight, especially when we have pressing family and work commitments. In my experience, the best way to make friends is to go out and find them rather than sitting and waiting for people to come and find you. One way is to be kind to women at work: random acts of kindness go a long way to laying the foundation of new friendships, and they tend to snowball. I now belong to an unofficial 'Friday fish and chips lunch club' that started when I reached out to one woman at work who was looking for friendship. After about 18 months, we hit on the idea of a fish and chip lunch in the newly refurbished canteen. A few lunches later, her colleague joined us. Soon, another woman I knew joined us because she was in the queue and had no one to sit with. The next Friday, I ended up having fish and chips with that woman and two others from her office. Now a regular 'ladies that lunch' email goes out each Friday morning, asking a steadily growing group of women if they are coming down for fish and chips! It's not doing our waistlines much good (I have offered to share a portion with someone) but it is good for friendship. So unless there is a very good reason, don't say 'No' when other women ask you to join them: the way we make friends is to join in.

Another way to make friends is to join in at church. I don't just mean going to church; I mean *doing something* with people from your fellowship. We recently got together to help an obsessive hoarder clear his house. It was like something from a TV show—rubbish piled floor to ceiling in every room of the house and in the backyard. One Saturday morning we filled two skips and brought light into the man's front room and into his life, but we also brought light into our own lives by forging bonds of friendship with people who had previously only been another face in the crowd. Coffee-time after services is much more fun once you have got to know people by working together.

I know from my past life in parish ministry that entertaining at home is also a good way to help build friendships. Asking people round can be risky, but, if you invite some old friends with some new ones, it can make the event go more smoothly. Knowing this, I decided that facing 50 was a great opportunity to have the birthday party of all parties: it would let me indulge my passion for cooking for crowds and give me the excuse to invite my friends, old and new, into our new home. I was shocked, though, at how difficult it was. First, I have fewer close friends than I thought, and second, I was surprised by the reticence of some of my new friends. Although two jumped enthusiastically at the thought, some took a long time even to mention that they had received the invitation. The evening went really well, but through it I learned that I am used to church culture, where people tend to be actively hospitable, and that many people who are not part of that kind of close community are not used to others opening their homes. Thus they may find it hard to accept the invitation. Nevertheless, it is good to persist, if for no other reason than that women in midlife who have good friends are happier, have fewer age-related ailments and are better able to withstand the detrimental effects of loss, including the loss of a spouse.[1] So, although I like my personal space and a busy schedule, I am going out of my way to build relationships in my new situation.

The issue of marriage at midlife is worth a book in its own right, and anything I say here can only scratch the surface, but it is undeniable that the changes and reassessments that men and women face during midlife can easily disrupt the delicate balances that both partners have worked so hard to keep in place over their years together. As far as I understand, a couple's response to those changes depends significantly on the investment they have made in their relationship in previous years, and, as such, relationships fall into a variety of categories. One marriage psychologist suggests four categories that characterise marriage at midlife:

- The competitive relationship, characterised by incessant struggle and mutual criticism.
- The boring relationship, in which staying with the other is merely a means of avoiding loneliness.
- The limited relationship, in which predictability and routine are actively embraced as a means of attaining security.
- The alert relationship, characterised by an ongoing interest in the other and a commitment to inner change and growth.[2]

I would like to think that my husband and I belong to the fourth group—couples who 'share an essential ability to retain an alert and fresh interest in each other... [who] whether together or alone are aware of each other, the way they are thinking and feeling, and their life is a joint experience of mutual productivity'.[3] It sounds wonderful, but this sort of relationship does not come easily or cheaply. As I have grown older, I have come to realise that 'women learn that to preserve their relationships, they must keep more and more of their reactions to themselves and take a path away from authenticity, mutuality and the truth of their experience'.[4] There is a lot that many women of my generation bury in a marriage relationship to keep the peace. For example, a woman may want her spouse to help out more with the housework when she has returned to work, but she is averse to making what might initially seem to be unreasonable demands. Many women just do both—a paid job and the housework—but that kind of arrangement will remain practical only for so long. The secret to authenticity in midlife and beyond is finding out how to let the real you, and your real needs, find expression without rocking the marital boat so much that it capsizes. (By the way, I get all the help I need in the house!)

As my husband has faced major change in his life due to leaving parish ministry, we have had many opportunities to talk through the changes we have both experienced at the emotional and spiritual level. Communicating at this kind of depth ensures that you change together and that you understand the experience your 'significant other' is going through. In the midst of all this change, it is important to provide reassurance that your love for each other remains. In this respect, we both find that reflecting on what we have to say before we say it, and picking a conducive moment, is the best way to ensure that what we need to communicate is understood in the way it was intended. Never forget that your spouse may be having to cope with as much change in their life as you are in yours, and sensitivity to each other's feelings and needs cannot be emphasised too highly.

Having shared some of my thoughts on aspects of relationships that we face in midlife, I am surprised to realise that, in some ways, I don't mind being the panini I decried at the beginning of this chapter. There may be pressure from both sides and some sour garnish in the middle, but at least life is interesting and provides a multitude of opportunities to explore my identity and get closer to the real me. I may not always like what I find, but the greatest treasure I have unearthed is a reminder that, like Naomi's kinsman-redeemer, the Lord 'renews our life and sustains us in our old age' (Ruth 4:14). I am ready to explore new aspects of that ultimate relationship. What about you?

Re-creation

- Take some time to examine your relationship with your parents, whether or not both of them are still alive. This could take more than one session and is likely to be a complex process, as your relationship with each one may have changed over the years. See if you can identify any unfulfilled dreams that they may have had for you. Do they match your own dreams, or have they held you back from developing a life of authenticity? What needs resolving or letting go? Could any of these old dreams form the basis for new creativity?
- It can be frightening to ask yourself honest questions about your marriage or your relationship with a significant other (I certainly don't like the trauma associated with the misunderstanding that can come from poorly expressed communication about feelings) but, if we are to be real people in the second half of our lives, we need to start asking real questions. Rather than presenting you with specifics, I suggest that you investigate giving your relationship an MOT in preparation for the years to come. There are books and courses available that can help.

- Children will always be a concern to their parents, however old they are. If you have children, take stock of your relationship. Are you holding any expectations over them that might prevent them developing in a direction more in line with their potential? Are there any skills you need to help them master before they can become fully independent? What can you do to transition your relationship with your child into one with a more adult foundation?
- Take a long look at your friends, or be prepared to admit your lack of them. Who are the ones you need to invest time in for the second half of life? Do you have the opportunity to make a conscious decision to make new friends or to let go of an unconstructive friendship? Do you need to join a social networking site to keep in touch?

Prayer

Lord, as I grow older, and even if I long for silence and solitude, I thank you that you made us beings who need one another. As my self and my circumstances change, help me to be the friend to others that I would wish to have as my own friend. Give me the selflessness and strength to nurture family relationships, and deepen the love I have for those to whom I am closest. Amen

For reflection

This third act—from the age of fifty on—can be the best act. If people know that you see them… that you hear them, that you are really taking them in, then you will never be without friends.[5]

As an older family member, you can give your family a sense of heritage, tradition and continuity that only your generation can provide.[6]

Chapter Five

A woman's work

Whatever your hand finds to do, do it with all your might,
for in the grave, where you are going, there is neither
working nor planning nor knowledge nor wisdom.

Ecclesiastes 9:10

The autumn term is over! The organisation I work for has
hit its annual targets and we have been rewarded with five
days' paid leave as part of our Christmas bonus. My festive
preparations are completed, and at last I am sitting at my
computer in the quiet of the conservatory, watching the
snow turn the chicken ark at the bottom of the garden into a
snug bivouac that would make Bear Grylls proud. So here I
am—the wrong side of 50, with ample opportunity to reflect
about the place of work in my life as I face up to the first year
of my 'second half'.

As I think about 'what I do', I realise that I have a plethora
of roles, some paid and some voluntary, some full-time and
some part-time. All of them define and reflect some aspect
of who I am and what my life experience has brought me:
wife, mother, housekeeper, gardener, caterer, writer, translator,
trustee of a charity, business support employee of a college
of further education and staff governor of the same—oh yes,
and a reserve fire marshal at the church I attend! Past roles
have included laboratory technician, part-time cleaner, part-
time barista (that's someone who works in a coffee shop, not

a court of law), company director, mature student and vicar's wife.

If you belong to my generation, it is quite likely that your track record is as chequered as mine. Thirty years ago, there were far fewer women, graduates or otherwise, who planned to have a career *and* a family. Those I knew personally who did try to have their cake and eat it had usually trained in one of the professions—doctor, dentist, lawyer or teacher—where there was a clear training and career structure to follow, and they pushed through to achieve it. In my early 20s I had shied away from trying to make my mark in the big wide world of work. Looking back, I think this was due to a combination of lack of self-confidence, indecision and a sneaking feeling that it was 'not quite the done thing' for a married Christian woman, because homemaking and supporting your husband were considered the norm. I had wanted to be a university lecturer in botany or mycology, but when the funding for the PhD programme I had hoped to follow was not approved by the relevant research council, I slipped quietly into a PGCE (although I never ended up teaching) and marriage to a clergyman in training. Not that I am complaining! As many of my current colleagues have commented, I have crammed a lot into my life compared to many others, but, despite the occasional admiration, somehow I am still left feeling that I have become a 'Jill-of-all-trades' and mistress of none.

I recently read an article about working mothers that ended with the comment, 'Mothers can have it all—just not all at once.'[1] In other words, you can have a family and be successful at work, but it's very hard to have both at the same time. All well and good, but, after 15 years of parenting, a woman in her late 40s most probably finds that the outside world has moved on without her and is reluctant to value her unique set of transferable skills. Think about it: when I had my first child, the Amstrad home computer was still a prototype and most people had never heard of the internet. If I had not decided to return to higher education when I turned 40 and sat through compulsory IT training, I would not have had the relevant skills to land a job as a student data administrator seven years later—even though organising four children takes a bundle of management skills. Admittedly, I returned to education not to learn IT, but to try to fulfil my ambition to be a university lecturer. The latter turned out not to be, but the IT skills have been of great benefit.

Looking round at the women I work with, I have come to the conclusion that career progression and taking a career break to raise children generally appear to be mutually exclusive, particularly if you measure success by rising to the most senior jobs. This observation seems to be supported by the findings of a recent survey of recruitment agencies specialising in top-salaried executives. Fifty three per cent of those recruiting for roles with a salary of £150K or more believed that a career break must be forsaken in order to attain such a high-level executive job.[2] Well, I've had that for a laugh, then: there will be no book entitled *Barefoot in the Boardroom*! In the light of such information, it is easy to become disheartened and think that you are destined to stay where you are until retirement—especially when you learn that the bulk of the administrative workers in the UK are women aged 40-plus. (Perhaps 'bulk' is an unfortunate word to use, considering the number of times dieting is the topic of conversation at work!)

As with so many situations in life, a work situation can be changed with the right attitude and a renewed perspective. I have already admitted my perfectionist tendencies, and I have always aimed to do my best in any job in any sphere of life: 'Whatever you do, work at it with all your heart, as working for the Lord' (Colossians 3:23). For example, a few years back, I was taking every opportunity to earn money, to help put down a deposit on our own home. Admittedly I was finishing my PhD thesis, but, to escape from my desk and get some exercise, I took a job cleaning a large house twice a week for a friend who ran a bed-and-breakfast business. It was back-breaking work changing six beds, ensuring that the four en suite bathrooms were left spotless and vacuuming what seemed like miles of corridors, but I enjoyed being left to my own devices and worked to provide an impeccable service. Apart from the excellent pay, my reward was to be publicly hailed by my employer, in church of all places, as 'the most qualified scrubber in the village'! What we do and how we do it may raise an eyebrow or even a laugh, but it's better that way than allowing our work to engender complaints and criticism.

I suppose, if I had been totally wholehearted about my renewed ambition to become a university lecturer, I would not have spent those two days a week working as a cleaner, but would rather have sweated over a series of academic articles, building up an impressive list of publications to boost my application for the post-doctoral research fellowship. Of course, it is important to do our best whatever our work, but it is also important that we are able to focus our activity on our main objective. Looking back, it might be fair to say that I thought I had identified my main objective—the research fellowship—whereas what I was subconsciously aiming for all along was a home of our own rather than the supposed job of my dreams. Now that we live in that home, I can confidently say that I am happy with the outcome of the last few years, although I was disappointed by losing the university job at the time.

Facing up to the second half of life is an opportunity to

take an honest look at our work aspirations and ask if our good ideas are actually 'God ideas'. I believe that God shut the door to university life for me because he knows the true desire of my heart and what really suits the way he has made me. Although I made the mistake of personalising the promise 'I have placed before you an open door that no one can shut' (Revelation 3:8) and believed that it was an assurance that my postgraduate studies would lead to a job at a university, I was obviously rattling the wrong door handle. I am sure there is still 'an open door that no one can shut' waiting for me to walk through—and it is possible that I have walked through it already without realising it—because, as Christians, we have the assurance that God 'knows the plans he has for us, plans to prosper us and not to harm us, plans to give us hope and a future' (see Jeremiah 29:11).

Sitting in my pastor's front room with a few other candidates for the church's early autumn newcomers' course, I was challenged to think about where I would like to be in ten years' time. I had been so busy moving house and settling into our new life that I'd had no time to think clearly about what lay ahead. Putting aside the highly improbable dream of one day owing a smallholding in Dorset with a view of the sea, I realised that a more practical dream would be to have fixed up our house (we need a new roof), established the garden (we are doing our version of *The Good Life* minus pig and goat), encouraged the children to have found places of their own (don't hold your breath) and paid off the mortgage (I said, don't hold your breath…) so that I can spend the quiet mornings writing novels and the afternoons pottering among the vegetables and talking to the chickens—once I am retired, mind you. That dream is a long way from the traditional notion of career success that I have carried around for the last ten years or so, and, although I was a bit shocked at my own honesty, the realisation was rather liberating. I was also challenged to think that we so easily get lost in the practical details of what we hope for our future that we forget God's 'big purposes' for us—to grow into the likeness of his Son, to deepen our wisdom and understanding of spiritual things, and to bring forth the fruit of the Spirit.

On reflection, I have learned the hard way that it is important to figure out the true desire of your heart, the desire that reflects the person you truly are in God, and to follow that dream. This realisation rarely happens overnight; for me, the process has taken almost three decades, and I wish I had come to it sooner. Having said that, I made a good attempt at achieving the writing / gardening / spiritual growth balance during our time in South Yorkshire in the late 1990s. Perhaps, back then, I should have jumped at the request from that American publisher to try my hand at a novel.

Once we have identified our dream, the risk is that we just sit and wait for it to happen, allowing opportunities to slip through our fingers or taking on projects that sidetrack us (which, you will realise by now, is my tendency). It is all very well being wholehearted, but we have to put our efforts into the right activities. I heard a sermon recently in which, yet again, Martha came in for criticism because she was too busy in the kitchen while Mary was in the front room sitting at Jesus' feet (see Luke 10:38–42). I would like to make it clear that I think *there is nothing wrong with being busy in the kitchen*—I love cooking and entertaining, and I would love to write a cookbook—and a general application of the unfavourable comparison of Martha's domestic activity with Mary's domestic passivity is not helpful. The story is actually a reminder that our efforts need to be focused on our main objective at the right time, and that we must not get sidetracked. Mary was busy, too, but in a different way: she was focused on what mattered most at that particular time. I'm sure she would have been helping in the kitchen if the guest of honour had not been Jesus. The point I am trying to make is this: if I want to be a successful writer and have a thriving garden, I am not going to get there by watching TV in my idle moments, ignoring creative ideas that pop into my head or taking a weekend job in a supermarket. My efforts need to be focused in the right place at the right time.

In the meantime, back in the present, I have a full-time job of work outside the home. Writing and gardening are confined to my spare time and are very much dependent on the seasons. Snow means a rug over my knees as I tap at a keyboard, and sunshine means that writing and translating are on hold while I weed the beans. The rest of the time, I sit at a computer in an open-plan office, doing whatever it is a timetabling officer in a college does all day long to ensure that 4500 students, 450 teaching staff, 28 laptop trolleys, a fleet of minibuses and a team of learning support workers are in the right place at the right time—and that's only the half of it. My day job is very different from what I thought I would be doing, and far from how I would wish to be spending my time—but, then, most of us live like that, if we are honest enough to admit it. Nevertheless, if we redefine our notion of success away from status within the organisation for which we work, or the financial reward we get for our efforts, I suspect that most of us are actually successful at what we do. When I look at my office job objectively, I never cease to be amazed at how well it suits the kind of person I am and my current domestic situation. I am highly organised, have an obsessive eye for detail and have to finish anything I've started—all necessary qualities in my role. My place of work is close to home, so I am still able to be on hand if there is a domestic emergency and I don't have to spend hours of my day commuting. It just goes to show that 'in all things God works for the good of those who love him, who have been called according to his purpose' (Romans 8:28), even if we don't quite understand why everything seems to be going 'wrong' sometimes.

So where do I go from here in terms of paid employment? Like a lot of women of my age, I need to get out of the house and do something constructive now that the children do not need me so much. I have always wanted to 'belong' and 'make a contribution', and I feel I am certainly doing that now. Some of us can afford our contribution to the wider world to be voluntary. I know of many women who do valuable work on a purely unpaid basis, and society would be at a loss without them. However, like many others, I need to work not just to keep my mind active and get out of the house, but because we need to pay for the house. For the woman of faith, a balance needs to be struck between having the assurance that God keeps everything in hand and will provide for us in future, and getting off our butts and working hard to ensure that our future needs are met. This delicate equilibrium between resting and striving has to be found in every area of life—whether it be doing what you can to help your children and trusting God to do the rest, or praying that the dinner you cooked for three mouths can be made to stretch to seven by more means than simply the judicious peeling of another pound of potatoes.

Getting a job, any job, can be hard enough when you have been based primarily at home in one capacity or another for a good many years, and the struggle to achieve it can lead to excessive striving. I have already admitted that I am competitive, I like to be the best at what I do, and I want to be in charge! In the past, these attributes have kept me up to the mark because I have worked in roles that required me to be self-motivated. I have been self-employed and also studying, competing against myself and meeting mainly self-imposed targets and deadlines. Put a mature person with those kinds of attributes into the workplace on the bottom rung of the corporate ladder, and they could have a problem—or, at least, have some major adjusting to do. Thankfully, much of my past devotional writing has focused on being real about ourselves and who we are in the sight of God, one of my favourite Bible passages being Philippians 2:3–7: 'Do nothing out of selfish ambition or vain conceit, but in humility consider others better than yourselves. Each of you should look not only to your own interests, but also to the interests of others. Your attitude should be the same as that of Christ Jesus, who… made himself nothing, taking the very nature of a servant.' Taking those words with me when I started back at 'work' helped me through the early days when the tasks I was given to do were mind-numbingly boring and repetitive. Even so, put in an unfamiliar environment, I found that there was much to learn and no place for a superior attitude.

Once I stopped struggling and striving to look for 'something better', I found an unfamiliar sense of contentment. As Kathleen Fischer so aptly puts it, 'part of the secret of satisfaction is giving up wishing you are doing something else'.[3] Nevertheless, knowing that you've 'arrived', so to speak, can lead to two reactions. You can start to feel demoralised by the thought that this is all there is and life is going to be the same predictable plod for the next 15 years, or you can give yourself permission to invest yourself in the organisation that employs you, even if there is the risk that it could cut you loose at any time due to the current economic climate.

The first attitude is all too common and not worthy of a woman of faith, because we are called to be 'salt and light' in the world (Matthew 5:13–16), to add value and make a difference rather than simply wondering what profit might be in it for us. The second attitude frees us to work from a place of rest, disentangles us from the power struggles going on around us, and enables us to be ourselves and bring all we have to our situation. It also allows us to grow. I have often trotted out 1 Peter 5:6–7 when our children have come home with worries from work: 'Humble yourselves, therefore, under God's mighty hand, that he may lift you up in due time. Cast all your anxiety on him because he cares for you.' These words are as pertinent to the 50-something restarter as they are to the 20-something new starter, but it can be a challenge to make them a reality in our lives, especially if we think that, at our age, we are cut out for more than *this*—'this' being the small task that we need to prove we can accomplish before we are given something more responsible.

Is there room for striving in the workplace? I think not. I am wont to agree with Anne Morrow Lindberg's sentiment that 'middle age is, or should be, a period of shedding shells: the shells of ambition... the shell of the ego'.[4] Nevertheless, although we may come to the conclusion that we are only a small cog in a large machine, there is always room for improvement, always more to learn and always more to give. Who knows, taking advantage of those learning and giving opportunities may prepare you for an opening you had no idea was in the offing. As I have written elsewhere many times before, one of my constant prayers is 'Lord, prepare me for what you are preparing for me.'[5] At 50-plus, there is still plenty to prepare ourselves for, plenty to invest in: 'Sow your seed in the morning, and at evening let not your hands be idle, for you do not know which will succeed, whether this or that, or whether both will do equally well' (Ecclesiastes 11:6).

Maintaining a value system that encourages us to work

from a place of rest (doing what we can and trusting in God's provision), rather than from striving (doing everything in our own strength and forgetting that God is faithful), flies in the face of the prevailing attitudes we may meet in the workplace. It can mean that we sometimes need to go against the general flow, even if that means being misunderstood. I have recently had to face this challenge. Over the last year, I have been on a management training course that began as an accredited certificate tailored by the training provider to meet the needs of my place of work. By the end of the year, pressure from others on the course resulted in the certificate being changed to a diploma, which would be recognised by other employers, if we submitted an extra three pieces of work. The problem was that some of us had already completed the assigned written work for the course, and I especially had counted on the whole thing being finished by December so that I could work on this book and a Norwegian translation. After much discussion, everybody except me decided that they were happy to do the three extra papers and obtain the diploma. I alone made it clear that I did not need a diploma recognised by other employers, as I was not looking to change my job. I could see that the others found this hard to understand, and I did have a slight twinge of panic that I might be seen as unwilling to put in the effort, but my reasons for doing the course were to benefit myself in my current place of work, not to provide myself with a springboard for going elsewhere. I may live to regret the decision, but it was important to me to stand by my commitment to grow in the place where I have been planted and to make time for my other writing commitments.

Where am I now in my thoughts about work? As I write, I am again sitting in the conservatory looking out on a snowy garden. As I contemplate the way ahead, the snow speaks to me of my future working life. It's not cold, barren, fruitless or dead, but a blazing blank canvas—a spacious place—upon which anything can be written, anything painted, anything built within the limits of imagination, opportunity, material resources, physical energy and, most importantly, the grace of God. The snowy garden is not flat. The snow is shaped by what lies beneath it and is blown into drifts by the wind. In the same way, the blank canvas of my future is already shaped by what has gone before. We can use the contours of our past to creative benefit in our future, for I believe that no experience, achievement, disappointment or failure is ever wasted.

A year ago, I would not have been able to write this chapter with the level of conviction that I can bring to it now. My work, both as an employee and as a freelance writer/translator, was fuelled by desperate striving, due to my 'unbridled sense of urgency to do something meaningful and achieve a level of success in the remaining years of my working life',[6] and with the added pressure of earning enough to pay off the mortgage in the next 18 years. Over the last twelve months, I have managed to redefine my understanding of meaningful work and career success. For all my earlier writing about simplicity and humility,[7] I realise that I had fallen into the trap of seeking worldly acclaim and financial reward. A week in France, digging my stepmother's garden while I waited for my father's funeral, had the same clarifying effect as a spiritual retreat. I came back to a place where I could again accept that I could do no more than my best and must trust God for the rest.

Undoubtedly there will be those around me, at work and in the local community, who will not understand my spirituality and the way it informs my values and choices, but what is important is that we are true to ourselves and what we believe, and that we demonstrate authenticity in the way we live out the remaining years of our lives. For me, returning to what I know to be true after a year or so of soul-searching has been the final lynchpin in the hinge to the door that has swung open to reveal a spacious place—the second half of life.

Re-creation

- Every woman works! Make an inventory of the jobs you do, whether they are voluntary or paid, your own choice or imposed upon you, either by unavoidable life circumstances or simply because you let life 'happen' rather than 'taking charge'.
- We all have jobs we can't get out of—often voluntary ones to do with our domestic circumstances. Despite having spent years trying to 'find God in the ordinary', my appetite for cleaning and ironing is wearing thin. I have three options: change my attitude, commandeer some help from other members of the household, or perhaps hire some help. Can you identify any such jobs in your life, which call for an innovative approach so that you are released to have more time and energy to become the person God intended you to be?
- Think about the jobs you do have a choice about. Are they what you want to be doing? Which ones would you change if you had the opportunity? Despite the current economic climate, there is no reason why you can't identify the kind of work you would rather be doing and prepare yourself for possible future opportunities. Update your CV or find someone to help you write one if you haven't got one already. Investigate any skills you might need to acquire

to get the kind of job you want, and look into possible avenues of training.[8]

- Ever thought of working for yourself? A hobby is something you spend money on, but a business is something that makes you money. It takes careful planning and hard work to turn a hobby or a good idea into a business, but many women have latent talents that can become fulfilling and profitable business propositions if approached correctly. I was my own boss for ten years and I loved every minute of it. It started with a few photocopied leaflets and a handful of advance orders that allowed me to purchase in the goods for my customers. After that, the business snowballed until it was eventually time to pass it into other hands.

Prayer

Lord, I give you my work in the home, in the marketplace and in the places where I volunteer. Reassure me if I am in the places where you have called me to be, or guide me clearly if I am not. In everything I do, help me to work as if I was working for you. Guard my heart from worldly ambition, teach me to serve, but prevent me from shying away from responsibility. Whether times are good or getting tough, help me to trust you, for I know we have no other help but you. Amen

For reflection

Often we hide out in comfy, unchallenging jobs that surround us with pleasant people, provide a pay cheque, and seem benign enough, except we are not expressing our authentic selves one tiny bit… when we deny parts of ourselves, we are limiting the options we have in life. There is an insidious link between hiding and self-sabotage.[9]

Ambitions are great. Change is essential. Dreams are necessary. But with it all, we find a greater peace if we hold on to a basic satisfaction with ourselves and life.[10]

Conclusion

Even to your old age and grey hairs,
I am he, I am he who will sustain you.
I have made you and I will carry you;
I will sustain you and I will rescue you.

Isaiah 46:4

'Will the real Alison please stand up!' Many times over the course of my early life, I heard my father say this to me. It was not spoken in jest or anger: in fact, I was too young to understand what he meant, so each time he asked, I was at a loss as to how to respond. I was as real as I could be at each of those moments, but, like many women, I didn't know what I wanted or who the real me might be. In some ways, it is sad that it has taken until now, when my father has passed away, for me to be able to say that the real me is standing up—albeit very shakily. Perhaps he had to go before I could find out who I really am: I just don't know. On the other hand, my husband would say that I have never been anything other than real, the whole time he has known me. I suspect he actually means honest and forthright, as I have always been one to tell it as it is. Nevertheless, there are times when I feel that, in some ways, I have spent most of my life on another planet and have only just come back down to earth, to an authentic reality. Apparently I am not the only one: Janis Fisher Chan expresses the same midlife experience when she asks, 'Do we become more conscious as we grow older? Sometimes it seems as if I've spent my life asleep and I am just now waking up.'[1]

As I made soup for lunch today, I dwelt on the thought of 'waking up'. Rather than thinking of *Sleeping Beauty*, I allowed my mind to be drawn to the story of Jairus' daughter (Luke 8:40–56). The twelve-year-old girl was sick. She died while Jesus was on his way to heal her, because he was delayed by another woman who also needed healing. When Jairus and Jesus reached the house, Jairus' servants told him not to bother Jesus because the girl was already dead. Jesus' response was to tell the father not to fear, because his daughter was not dead but asleep. In the child's room with three of his disciples, Jesus took her by the hand and told her to get up. We are told that 'her spirit returned, and at once she stood up' (v. 55); then Jesus told her parents to give her something to eat.

I hope I am not drawing too much out of the story, but it seems to me that here is a parallel with women's lives. As children, we are alive, well and, all being as it should be, not bothered by the cares of the world, but we are very present in our own reality. At twelve years old, around the time when the hormones kick in, it is as if we enter another world, succumbing to a deep sleep from which we cannot be awakened. Whether we call it peer pressure, cultural and social expectations or just our biological make-up, unless we are very strong-minded, it seems hard to escape. If midlife can be a time of awakening consciousness and a renewing of spirituality, the raising of Jairus' daughter may be an apt representation. Jesus describes the girl as sleeping, which, in some ways, sounds to me like an appropriate description of the last 30–40 years of my life.

Jesus takes the dead girl by the hand and tells her to stand up. Despite the fact that our outward appearance will have changed over the years, the girl inside us is suddenly alive and present again, with the same sense of wonder at the world around, but now with a deeper sense of wisdom and insight. I do not think I could put my finger on a specific point in my life over the last year when Jesus took me by the hand and told me to stand up, but the ongoing process of being touched by his Spirit means that I am on my feet, admittedly rather dazed but certainly back in reality and ready to get on with my life.

Preachers I have heard speak on this passage have always made much of Jesus' compassion and awareness of our physical needs, because he asks for the awakened girl to be given something to eat. In the Bible, food is often used as a symbol of the abundant life that God offers us if we live in relationship with him: for example, 'Here I am! I stand at the door and knock. If anyone hears my voice and opens the door, I will come in and eat with him, and he with me' (Revelation 3:20). This brings me full circle, back to one of the verses I quoted at the beginning of this book, a verse in which food (God's abundant life) and the idea of 'a spacious place' are equated: 'He is wooing you from the jaws of distress to a spacious place free from restriction, to the comfort of your table laden with choice food' (Job 36:16).

At the moment, I can only glimpse a little of what 'the spacious place' of the second half of my life holds for me. I have hinted at some of the things I would like to happen, and I hope they are on the 'table laden with choice food' before me. Nevertheless, I am now old enough and wide enough (sorry, wise enough) to know that we may have one set of plans but God may have another. The key is to listen more clearly, more authentically and more fearlessly. I will certainly finish my vegetable garden and potager—body willing—but maybe, by this time next year, I'll be working in a different job for a different organisation, and in ten years' time I'll wonder why I ever wanted to be a writer because life will have taken an unexpected turn. But for now I have my dreams and I am waiting for God's direction. As always, and maybe now more than ever, I try to live by the verse I was given at my baptism in 1988: 'Trust in the Lord with all your heart and lean not on your own understanding; in all your ways acknowledge him, and he will make your paths straight' (Proverbs 3:5–6).

I am very much aware that in this book I have not provided a clear set of answers or a list of step-by-step instructions for women at midlife. This is mainly because there are too many questions—and, besides, we are all so different in terms of our identity and life circumstances. When it comes to complex issues, we must make up our own minds and pursue the process of change for ourselves.[2] However, I do realise that many women's lives are fraught with a variety of challenges and difficulties, and that although we may want time to ourselves to pursue our own goals, this may not be possible due to changing demands within the family.[3]

Despite the variety of challenges that face us in our everyday lives (and I, too, have my fair share of those), I hope and pray that the second half of life will afford you the opportunity to be all that God intended you to be. You may not agree with some of what I have written. That is your prerogative and you should weigh up everything carefully, but I hope that my being vulnerable and honest in sharing my thoughts and experiences will persuade you to take a fresh look at your life, encouraging you to put your hand in the hand of Christ and live the remainder of your life in the fullness that he intended.

May the God of peace… equip you with everything good for doing his will, and may he work in us what is pleasing to him, through Jesus Christ, to whom be glory for ever and ever. Amen
HEBREWS 13:20–21

Notes

Introduction

1   Leslie Bennetts, 'Don't give up the day job', *Times 2*
    (2 April 2007).
    http://women.timesonline.co.uk/tol/life_and_style/
    women/article1560007.ece
2   Alie Stibbe, 'Looking back, looking forward', *New Wine
    Magazine*, Issue 1 (Spring 1997), p. 12.
3   Grant Luton, *In His Own Words: Messianic Insights into the
    Hebrew Alphabet* (Beth Tikkun, 1999), pp. 89–98.
4   Wilhelm Gesenius, *A Hebrew and English Lexicon of
    the Old Testament*, translated from Latin by Edward
    Robinson DD (Crocker and Brewster, 1836), p. 937.
    www.htmlbible.com/sacrednamebiblecom/kjvstrongs/
    STRHEB47.htm
5   Charles B. Bugg, *Preaching and Intimacy: Preparing the
    Message and the Messenger* (Smyth & Helwys, 1999),
    p. 67.
6   http://commons.wikimedia.org/wiki/File:Moses_%26_
    Bush_Icon_Sinai_c12th_century.jpg. This link shows an
    image of the icon of Moses and the burning bush that I
    used for meditational purposes when writing *Barefoot in
    the Kitchen*.
7   www.myjewishlearning.com/holidays/Jewish_Holidays/
    Passover/Themes_and_Theology/Self-Liberation.shtml
8   Adrian Hastings, Alistair Mason and Hugh S. Pyper,
    'Exile' in *The Oxford Companion to Christian Thought*
    (Oxford University Press US, 2000), p. 227.

Chapter One

1 'Hot flushes, memory loss linked in midlife women', IANS (17 June 2008). www.thaindian.com/newsportal/health/hot-flushes-memory-loss-linked-in-midlife-women_10061172.html

2 'Tips for keeping a keen memory in midlife'. www.amidlifecrisis.co.uk/tips-for-keeping-a-keen-memory-in-midlife.html

3 Timothy K. Jones, 'Reading life backwards', *Christianity Today* (22 September 1989).

4 Elie Wiesel, 'Hope, despair and memory', Nobel Lecture (11 December 1986). www.english.illinois.edu/maps/holocaust/wiesel.htm

5 Cathryn Jakobson Ramin, 'In search of lost time', *New York Times* (5 December 2004). www.nytimes.com/2004/12/05/magazine/05MEMORY. html?_r=1&pagewanted=1&ei=5089&en=62b57a10 bd76ee67&ex=1259989200&partner=rssyahoo

6 Marshall Hawkins, 'Reading our lives'. www.uuworld. org/spirit/articles/23892.shtml

7 Liz Perkins, 'Exploring new paths: emotional and spiritual growth for women at midlife'. www.midlifeandmenopause.co.uk/exploring.html

8 Ellen M. Ross, 'Spiritual experience and women's autobiography: the rhetoric of self-hood in the Book of Margery Kempe', *Journal of the American Academy of Religion*, 59.3 (OUP, 1991), pp. 527–546.

9 Jones, 'Reading life backwards'.

10 A. Amarasingam, 'Do not forget the Lord Your God', *Jewish Magazine* (June 2007), www.jewishmag.com/114mag/memory/memory.htm

11 www.famousquotes.com/category/unsorted/651

12 http://www2.eng.cam.ac.uk/~tpl/texts/dante.html (see the translation example by Tozer)

13 Jones, 'Reading life backwards'.

14 Anne Lamott, *Bird by Bird: Some Instructions on Writing and Life* (Anchor, 1994), p. xxiii.

Chapter Two

1 Erica James, *Tell It to the Skies* (Orion, 2007), p. 338.

2 Alie Stibbe, 'The key to inner healing', *Renewal* 215 (April 1994), pp. 33–35.

3 Alie Stibbe, in 'How the other half lives', *Christianity* (December 2010), p. 24.

4 Anita Renfroe, 'Wrinkled Ladies', music video: www.youtube.com/watch?v=bYpPDG6W-94

5 Nancy Gibbs, 'Midlife crisis? Bring it on!', *Time* (8 May 2005).
www.time.com/time/magazine/
article/0,9171,1059032,00.html

6 Janny E. Adkins, 'The midlife woman: the call to authenticity'. www.tidesoflife.com/midlife_woman.htm

7 Miriam Stoppard, 'How to deal with a midlife crisis', *Daily Mirror* (10 April 2009).

8 Dana King, Melissa H. Hunter, Jerri R. Harris, 'Spiritual issues facing women at midlife', Chapter 7 in *Dealing with the Psychological and Spiritual Aspects of Menopause: Finding Hope in the Midlife* (Haworth Pastoral, 2005), p. 76, quoting J.W. Pennebaker and J.D. Seagal, 'Forming a story: the health benefits of narrative', *Journal of Clinical Psychology* 55(10), pp. 1243–1254.

9 'Lisa', anonymous midlife female blogger discussing the goals of old age: http://lifetwo.com/production/node/20100105-what-goal-old-age

10 Marie Dressler, www.canadaka.net/modules.
    php?name=Famous_Canadians&action=viewperson&
    person=251

Chapter Three

1   Ernest Jones, *The Life and Work of Sigmund Freud*, Vol. 1
    (Basic Books, 1953), Chapter 1.
2   Linda N. Edelstein, *The Art of Midlife: Courage and
    Creative Living for Women* (Bergin & Garvey, 1999), p.
    123.
3   Pamela D. Blair, *The Next Fifty Years: A Guide for Women
    at Midlife and Beyond* (Hampton Roads, 2005), p. 127.
4   Grace Shepherd, *An Aspect of Fear* (DLT, 1989).
5   Blair, *The Next Fifty Years*, p. 115.
6   King, Hunter and Harris, 'Spiritual issues facing women
    at midlife', p. 81.
7   Peter Brierley, 'Female church goers', *Church of England
    Newspaper* (19 October 2007).
8   Kathleen Fischer, *Moving On: A Spiritual Journey for
    Women of Maturity* (SPCK, 1995), p. 1.
9   Fischer, *Moving On*, p. 2.
10 Allison Pearson, *Good Housekeeping* (June 2003).
11 Margaret Young: www.brainyquote.com/quotes/
    authors/m/margaret_young.html. (Margaret Young was
    an American jazz singer in the early 20th century.)

Chapter Four

1   Blair, *The Next Fifty Years*, pp. 227–228.
2   Jack Dominian, 'Married life' in Beatrice Musgrave and
    Zoe Menell (eds), *Change and Choice: Women and Middle
    Age* (Peter Owen, 1980), pp. 73–76.
3   Dominian, 'Married life', p. 75.

4   Blair, *The Next Fifty Years*, p. 108.

5   Nancy Friday, *The Power of Beauty* (Hutchinson, 1996), quoted in Blair, *The Next Fifty Years*, p. 224.

6   Eudora Seyfer, *How to be Happily Retired* (Celestial Arts, 1995), quoted in Blair, *The Next Fifty Years*, p. 222.

Chapter Five

1   Sandra Parsons, 'Mothers CAN have it all (just not all at once)', *Daily Mail* (21 July 2010), p. 15.

2   Claire Finney, 'No, my mother wasn't there at the school gate; she was there when it mattered', *Optima*, Vol. 457 (20 November 2010), p. 63.

3   Fischer, *Moving On*, p. 68.

4   Anne Morrow Lindberg, *Gift from the Sea* (Pantheon, 2003).

5   This is a prayer of Corrie ten Boom, which I found stuck to a cupboard door when we moved into a house previously occupied by one of her former travelling companions, Ellen de Kroon-Stamps.

6   Blair, *The Next Fifty Years*, p. 251.

7   Alie Stibbe, 'Humility', in *Day by Day with God* May–August 1998 (BRF, 1998); 'Oh, for a quiet and simple life', *New Wine Magazine*, Issue 8 (Winter 1998), p. 21; 'Psalms: living in God's presence', in *Day by Day with God* May–August 2006 (BRF, 2006); 'Contentment', *Day by Day with God* September–December 2011 (BRF, 2011).

8   There are quite a few books that help women make career choices at midlife, whether they are returning after a break or wanting to do something completely different after 'half-time'. One book I have found helpful, although it is written for the American market,

is Jan Cannon, *Now What Do I Do? The Woman's Guide to a New Career* (Capital, 2005).

9   Blair, *The Next Fifty Years*, p. 126.
10 Edelstein, *The Art of Midlife*, p. 115.

Conclusion

1   Janis Fisher Chan, *Inventing Ourselves Again: Women Face Middle Age* (Sibyl, 1996), p. 196.
2   William Bridges, *Transitions: Making Sense of Life's Changes* (Da Capo, 2004), pp. 157–161.
3   Laura Airey, 'Women in their fifties: well-being, ageing and anticipation of ageing', *CRFR Research Briefing* 24 (University of Edinburgh, September 2005).

Also by Alie Stibbe

Barefoot in the Kitchen

Bible readings and reflections for mothers

Here is a book of short Bible-based reflections for every mother who has ever felt that parenting young children is something of a desert time.

Drawing on her writing from *Day by Day with God* Bible reading notes (BRF/Christina Press), among other sources, author Alie Stibbe shares her own story and some of the ways she discovered of finding God in the most mundane of everyday tasks. Even when we are 'barefoot in the kitchen', we may in fact be standing on holy ground!

Despite the difficulties—even desolation—that we may pass through in the course of our journey, Alie shows that God is faithful to his word and will bring us to the promised land in the end.

ISBN 978 1 84101 346 6   £7.99
To order a copy of this book, please visit www.brfonline.org.uk.

Rhythms of Grace

Finding intimacy with God in a busy life

Tony Horsfall

Rhythms of Grace emerges from a personal exploration of contemplative spirituality. Coming from an evangelical and charismatic background, Tony Horsfall felt an increasing desire to know God more deeply. At the same time, he felt an increasing dissatisfaction with his own spiritual life, as well as concern at the number of highly qualified and gifted people involved in Christian ministry who experience burn-out.

In this book he shows how contemplative spirituality, with its emphasis on realising our identity as God's beloved children and on being rather than doing, has vital lessons for us about discovering intimacy with God. It also provides essential insights about building a ministry that is both enjoyable and sustainable.

ISBN 978 1 84101 842 3   £7.99
To order a copy of this book, please visit www.brfonline.org.uk.

Shaping the Heart

Reflections on spiritual formation and fruitfulness

Pamela Evans

God created the human heart to be a worship-filled, holy place with himself in residence, a garden in which the fruit of the Spirit may grow. *Shaping the Heart* is a book for every Christian who wants their heart to become—through the healing and redemptive touch of heavenly grace and mercy—a place where God delights to dwell.

Shaping the Heart is designed for practical use, whether as individual reading for a retreat or quiet day or for shared study and discussion in a group setting. The book considers different aspects of our lives in the light of Christian teaching and looks at how God can touch and transform us through his Spirit, so that we become fruitful disciples. Chapters conclude with three Bible reflections as a springboard to further prayer and reflection.

ISBN 978 1 84101 726 6   £7.99
To order a copy of this book, please visit www.brfonline.org.uk.

Discovering the Spiritual Exercises of Saint Ignatius

Larry Warner

This book is an adaptation of the Spiritual Exercises of St Ignatius Loyola, to help you to embark on a life-transforming journey toward Christlikeness. For nearly 500 years, the Exercises have been a tool for spiritual formation. During those years their popularity has ebbed and flowed, but they are now experiencing something of a revival across the breadth of the Church.

This is not a book about the methods or techniques of Christian formation but one that enables you to come before God through the Gospel narratives in order to encounter Jesus afresh. If you hunger for something deeper, yearn to walk with Jesus (not just read about him) and desire to embrace more of what God is doing in and through you, then this is the book for you.

ISBN 978 1 84101 883 6   £10.99
To order a copy of this book, please visit www.brfonline.org.uk.

Writing the Icon of the Heart

In silence beholding

Maggie Ross

In *Writing the Icon of the Heart* we are invited to share the reflections of one who, over the years, has spent long hours in silence and prayer in one of the world's most wild and solitary landscapes, as well as the more urban context of Oxford. Casting new and often startling light on ancient texts and long-established spiritual practices, Maggie Ross shows how faith cannot be divorced from an outlook characterised by a rigorous questioning and testing of assumptions, and a passionate concern for the created world in which we are blessed to live.

This is a book that challenges as well as inspires, and takes us deep into what it truly means to worship, to love, to pray—and to be human, made in the image of God.

ISBN 978 1 84101 878 2   £6.99
To order a copy of this book, please visit www.brfonline.org.uk.

Enjoyed

this book?

Write a review–we'd love to hear what you think.
Email: reviews@brf.org.uk

Keep up to date–receive details of our new books as they happen.
Sign up for email news and select your interest groups at:
www.brfonline.org.uk/findoutmore/

Follow us on Twitter @brfonline

By post–to receive new title information by post (UK only), complete the form below and post to: BRF Mailing Lists, 15 The Chambers, Vineyard, Abingdon, Oxfordshire, OX14 3FE

Your Details
Name _____
Address_____
_____
Town/City _____ Post Code _____
Email_____

Your Interest Groups (*Please tick as appropriate)	
❏ Advent/Lent	❏ Messy Church
❏ Bible Reading & Study	❏ Pastoral
❏ Children's Books	❏ Prayer & Spirituality
❏ Discipleship	❏ Resources for Children's Church
❏ Leadership	❏ Resources for Schools

Support your local bookshop
Ask about their new title information schemes.